★ FORREST'S ★
FIGHTING
PREACHER

DAVID CAMPBELL KELLEY *of* TENNESSEE

★ ★ ★ ★ ★ ★ ★ ★ ★ ★ ★ ★ ★ ★ ★ ★ ★

MICHAEL R. BRADLEY

THE
History
PRESS

Published by The History Press
Charleston, SC 29403
www.historypress.net

Front cover: Image of Nathan Bedford Forrest courtesy of the Gladstone Archive of African
American Photographs.

All images are by the author unless otherwise noted.

First published 2011
Manufactured in the United States
ISBN 978.1.60949.383.7

Library of Congress Cataloging-in-Publication Data
Bradley, Michael R. (Michael Raymond), 1940-
Forrest's fighting preacher : David Campbell Kelley of Tennessee / Michael R. Bradley.
p. cm.
Includes bibliographical references and index.
ISBN 978-1-60949-383-7
1. Kelley, D. C. (David Campbell), 1833-1909. 2. Forrest, Nathan Bedford,
1821-1877--Friends and associates. 3. Confederate States of America. Army. Cavalry-
-Officers--Biography. 4. Soldiers--Confederate States of America--Biography. 5.
Methodist Church--Tennessee--Clergy--Biography. 6. Tennessee--History--Civil War,
1861-1865--Campaigns. 7. United States--History--Civil War, 1861-1865--Campaigns.
8. Tennessee--History--Civil War, 1861-1865--Biography. 9. United States--History--Civil
War, 1861-1865--Biography. I. Title.
E467.1.K29B72 2011
973.7'82092--dc23
[B]
2011024051

This book is dedicated to
My grandson
Michael Alexander Warren

The descendant of a Confederate cavalryman
Elias F. Alexander
1st South Carolina Cavalry

Contents

CONTENTS

Acknowledgements

Thanks to:

Knox Martin, chief genealogist, Tennessee Division, Sons of Confederate Veterans, Memphis, Tennessee.

Brian Hogan, Researcher, Tennessee Valley Civil War Roundtable, Huntsville, Alabama.

Ronnie Mangrum, member, Sons of Confederate Veterans, Franklin, Tennessee, for providing me with the Corder Manuscript, an unpublished account of a reunion of a small group of Confederates held in 1922 at a family home.

Harriet Vivian, volunteer at the archives of the United Methodist Church, Nashville, Tennessee.

Von Unruh, former archivist with the United Methodist Church, Nashville, Tennessee.

Hargrett Library Rare Books and Manuscripts staff, University of Georgia.

Perkins Library Rare Books and Manuscript staff, Duke University.

ACKNOWLEDGEMENTS

Steve Settle, Sons of Confederate Veterans, Dover, Tennessee; chair of Friends of Fort Donelson Battlefield.

Jimmy Settle, Sons of Confederate Veterans, historian, Fort Donelson Memorial Chapel.

Martha Bradley, who drew the maps and supported me in every way during this project.

Chapter 1

Before the War

FAMILY BACKGROUND

Christmas Day 1833 was a special time of celebration in the little Wilson County, Tennessee community called by some Stringtown and by others Kelley's Church. The usual holiday festivities were supplemented in the house of the Reverend Mr. John Kelley and his wife, Margaret Livinia Campbell Kelley, by the birth of a son. Named David, the infant was soon baptized as a member of the little Methodist congregation to which his father was pastor.

Wilson County was scarcely two generations away from being a raw frontier. The first white settlers had come to nearby Nashville in 1780. The stories of fights with the local Native Americans were still recent memories, and the word "station" as part of a place name did not indicate the stopping place for railway trains but, rather, was a reminder that the location was the site of a frontier fortification. The year David Campbell Kelley was born was the semi-centennial of the Revolutionary War, which had ended in 1783 and in which both his grandfathers had fought.

John Kelley was the son of Dennis Kelley and Elizabeth Thompson, and Dennis was still alive when his grandson David was born. Dennis had been born on August 25, 1758, and had lived for many years in Sussex County, Delaware. As a teenage boy, he had joined the Continental army and had served as one of the guards of the British spy Major John André, who had been apprehended with letters from Benedict Arnold. Dennis had married Elizabeth Thompson in 1784, and sometime after that the couple had moved to what would become Tennessee to take advantage of the good lands offered to Revolutionary veterans. Grandfather Dennis would live until December 11, 1834, so David would have no actual memory of his Revolutionary sire, but his stories would be told in the family for many years to come.[1]

The grandfather for whom David was named was dead when the child was born, having passed away in August 1832. He was David Campbell, one of the descendants of "Black Dave" Campbell, a legendary frontiersman from Virginia. Grandfather David was born near Abingdon, Virginia, on August 18, 1753. He had been a soldier in Lord Dunmore's War (1774) and had moved to the Wautauga Settlements in what is now east Tennessee when the Revolution broke out. During the War for Independence, David fought at the Battles of Long Island Flats in 1776 and at Kings Mountain in 1780. He was a captain in the Territorial Militia, served as a member of the assembly for the abortive State of Franklin and then became a major in the Tennessee militia and rose to the rank of lieutenant colonel. When Tennessee became a state in 1796, David Campbell was elected as a member of the Tennessee General Assembly.

David Campbell had moved from the Wautauga Settlements to the vicinity of modern Knoxville in 1785. He built a stockade to protect his farmhouse, and the settlement that grew up around it was named Campbells Station, today a suburb of Knoxville. On the death of his first wife, a cousin named Margaret Campbell, in 1799, David remarried, this time to Jane Montgomery Cowan. The couple had four children, but only one, Margaret Lavinia Campbell, lived to adulthood. In 1823, David and Jane moved to Wilson County to settle on six hundred acres of land, becoming neighbors of Dennis and Elizabeth Kelley and their son John. At this time, Margaret Lavinia was nineteen and John Kelley was twenty-one. The neighbors became husband and wife. Although Grandfather David died before his grandson was born, Grandmother Jane lived until 1840 and told her grandson the stories of his legendary ancestors.[2]

John Kelley was a respected member of the Tennessee Conference of the Methodist Episcopal Church. There was no Methodist church in Stringtown when John arrived there, but he organized a congregation that met under an oak tree. John Buchanan, a member of the church, gave some land for the congregation to use for a building site, but that property became the cemetery. A building was eventually erected on an adjacent lot and was named Pleasant Grove Methodist Church. John Kelley served the little congregation at Stringtown faithfully, working not only in the service of the church but also supporting education in the community. Indeed, John served the congregation and the community so loyally the town was often called "Kelley's Church." His wife, Margaret Lavinia, was equally devout and was active in opening new areas of service for women in the church. She became the founder of one of the first mission societies in the Methodist Church in Tennessee.[3]

The community where David Campbell Kelley would spend his childhood was typical of hundreds of American communities of the time. The hamlet was surrounded by fertile farmland, and most people got their living from the soil. Nearby Hickory Ridge provided woods for hunting, and Cedar Lick Creek was a good place to fish as well as providing the water power for a gristmill. Like every such community of the time, it had a general store and a blacksmith shop where repairs to farm tools could be made and where the smith also worked as a farrier. The Methodist church was the center of the social and spiritual life of the community.[4]

In this developing society, the Methodist church and the Kelley family both prospered. John Kelley purchased land and went into farming to supplement his income from his duties as a minister. Eventually he would own over two hundred acres of land and would hold six slaves. John Kelley called his farm Long View. Some of the slaves worked the land, but at least one woman labored as cook and housekeeper to assist Margaret. A good part of the Kelley land was used for grazing horses and mules, cattle and sheep. The row crops were corn and wheat, which provided food for both the livestock and the people who lived on the property. The proximity of the Kelley farm to Nashville meant there was a ready market for their livestock. The Kelleys had good relations with their slaves. All six were still living on the farm as the Civil War drew to an end despite the fact that the U.S. Army had occupied the area in 1862 and held Nashville continuously until the end of the conflict.

The income from the church, coupled with the produce of the farm, placed the Kelleys in the upper middle class. Only some 10 percent of heads of families in the South owned slaves, according to the 1860 census, and John Kelley was part of this economic group. However, the ownership of a couple of hundred acres of land and six slaves makes Kelley a typical small operator, better off financially than those who farmed with only the labor of their own family but most certainly not a "planter" who was supported by the labor of slaves. Margaret and her husband both had to work every day to maintain their family's financial stability.

David Campbell Kelley would grow up in a home where religion was the central focus, where education was valued and where a good family income provided him opportunities not available to many. All these things involved the necessity to work on his part both for financial and moral reasons. It was part of the family creed that the Epistle of James should be followed—"he who does not work shall not eat."

Growing up in a rural area, David knew all the country pleasures of hunting, fishing and horseback riding. But his education was not neglected. In a pattern typical for his time, place and social class David was taught by a succession of tutors who maintained small neighborhood schools. This teaching was supplemented by home schooling, as his parents assigned him various texts to read.

EDUCATION

In the summer of 1848, David went on an extended visit to Montcalm, the Campbell family home near Abingdon, Virginia. While on this family visit, David wrote home to tell his parents that he had visited Emory & Henry College to see if he might like to study there. He had made an interesting and educational visit to the salt works at Saltville and was continuing his reading program by perusing Prescott's *Conquest of Mexico*. This history of the Spanish conquest was not only a classic of nineteenth-century historical writing, but it also fitted the current interest in the nation with which the United States had just concluded a war. Neither was David neglecting his spiritual development. He wrote that he had attended church every Sunday since his arrival in Virginia; he had attended the Episcopal church twice, the Methodist church twice and had once gone to the Presbyterian service.[5]

Like all parents, John and Margaret Kelley were concerned about their teenage son's behavior toward young women. David Campbell wrote from Montcalm to assure the Kelleys that a letter they had received concerning David was rather overstated. David Campbell assured the parents that his nephew, David Kelley, had "not been playing the beau with the young women of Abingdon." The teen was characterized by his uncle as being "genteel" and "intellectual."[6]

David had a good relationship with his younger sister Mary. Although he sent her greetings in his letters to his parents, he did not neglect to write to her personally. One such letter describes his trip from Lebanon to the Campbell relatives at Campbells Station near Knoxville and then on to Abingdon.

The members of the party had taken turns riding in a carriage and riding horseback. On many occasions, the passengers in the carriage had to get out and walk to lighten the load for the horses as they went up some of the steeper ridges. Sometimes the horses needed to rest so often that the walkers got to the top first. Every day, the journey was broken with a midday picnic at a spring or on the banks of a creek. The most interesting stop overnight had been at Beersheba Springs atop a mountain near McMinnville, Tennessee. David described the inn as "standing on the brow of a precipice."[7]

In early September 1858, David Kelley was nearing the end of his visit to Montcalm. He wrote his mother that a party of family members was planning their journey to Lebanon. In the meantime, he was reading the New Testament every morning and then taking a walk. The rest of the time before dinner at 1:00 p.m. was spent in conversation with the members of the extensive Campbell family. In the afternoons, he read history from the classics. The afternoon concluded with a horseback ride or a walk.[8]

On returning to Itinerants Rest that fall of 1848, David enrolled at Cumberland College in Lebanon, Tennessee. Although not an old institution, Cumberland had already established a reputation for academic excellence. Because the college was only a short horseback ride from his home, there

Beersheba Springs Hotel, where David Kelley stopped on his way to Virginia.
Courtesy Library of Congress.

is no surviving correspondence that gives an insight into his experiences there. What is obvious is that during his undergraduate years, David made a commitment that shaped the rest of his life. At some time, David understood that he was called to a religious vocation; he would dedicate his life to being a minister. It is reasonable to assume that the young man discussed the matter with his parents and received their proud approval.

For David, his initial sense of call was to go to China as a missionary. The Methodist Episcopal Church, South, like many other evangelical Protestant churches, had developed an intense interest in China. The Opium Wars, initiated by Great Britain, as well as the influx of Chinese to America during the California Gold Rush, had made Christians in the United States aware of the millions in that country who had never heard the Christian gospel. The response was to found societies to raise money to send preachers to China. Margaret Kelley, David's mother, had begun one such society. Her influence on his decision to become a missionary may have been considerable.

David decided to take more than preaching skills to China; he resolved to become a medical doctor as well. In 1852, after graduating from Cumberland College, David enrolled in the medical department of the University of Nashville. This school was beginning to make a name for itself regionally.

Medical study was not beyond David's mental ability, but he did not find appealing that part of his work that depended heavily on memorization. He did see parallels with other of his studies. David wrote to a friend that his study of anatomy in the dissection laboratory provided for him an "incontrovertible argument in favor of a designer and creator of wisdom having accomplished this work," *i.e.*, the human body.[9]

David also had time to comment on current events. Writing to his family, he noted that the deaths of Daniel Webster and Henry Clay had been received in Nashville and that ceremonies honoring both men had been conducted. Clay, David felt, was "mourned with the heart, Webster with the head." Henry Clay had died on June 29, 1852; Webster on October 24. In typical college student fashion, the same letter that noted the passing of two national leaders of legendary status also spoke of how pleased David was with the corndodgers his mother had recently sent by a friend who had traveled from Lebanon to Nashville. The treat had been shared with Joe, one of the Kelley slaves who had been sent to Nashville with David as a body servant.[10]

A news-filled letter just a week before Christmas recounted more details about student life in medical school. Some students, David recounted, fainted during the classes where they observed surgery. Personally, he was not bothered by the process. He also noted that he was finding opportunities to practice the ministerial part of his dual profession, as he received many invitations to preach.

One such invitation had just been fulfilled at McKendree Methodist Church, then, as now, one of the largest Methodist churches in Nashville and the "mother church" of the denomination with its location downtown on Church Street and its history stretching back to the early days of Nashville. The novice preacher said it was a rainy night and "only a few were present," which "relieved my embarrassment."

Part of that embarrassment was because medical study did not leave David enough time to make what he considered adequate preparation for entering the pulpit. As a result, David said he had decided to "preach in a general style without focusing closely on a topic." This, he felt, would be acceptable so long as he had a new audience each time! As an aside, David said Joe would like some ham to go with the next batch of corn bread his mother sent.[11]

MARRIAGE AND MISSIONS

Study was not the only thing on David's mind. He had decided he needed a wife. Since he did not know any young women who were inclined to accompany him to China, he went looking for one! In September 1853, he wrote his mother from Columbia, Tennessee. David had met the Reverend Mr. W.E. Johnson, a Methodist minister from Columbia, and Mr. Johnson had offered to introduce David to some young women of his congregation who had expressed sympathy for the cause of missions in China. After meeting them, David found their sympathy did not extend to wishing to go to China as his wife. Not discouraged, David had decided to go farther south. In his letter, David made it clear that he was at odds with his father, who did not think David should marry at that time, but David asserted that he would think for himself on the matter and his mind was made up.[12]

David continued his journey to Florence, Alabama, in the company of a Methodist preacher he identified as "Brother Mirrell." From Florence, David wrote his mother that he was still looking for a wife and that he had no intention of going to China as an unwed man. He was planning to go from Florence to Oxford, Georgia, the site of a Methodist college, Emory. Although he did not have much money, David said, he was "traveling Methodist preacher style," staying with church members who invited him to spend a day or so with them, and that he could travel a good many more days if necessary.[13]

The trip to Georgia was never made. While at Florence, David met a young woman from the nearby village of Waterloo, Alabama. Manerva Amanda Harris would become Mrs. David C. Kelley on January 4, 1854.[14] In 1880, one of David and "Mannie's" daughters, Lizzie Mannie Kelley, speculated that:

> *I very much doubt whether Papa was ever violently in love as is correct for all novel heroes to be. His courtship was short. He had decided to go to China and did not wish to go single. Someone mentioned my mother to him as a pious suitable young lady for a missionary's wife. He went to see her and with some difficulty persuaded my Grandmother Harris to allow him to take her favorite child so far from her, for she never expected to see her again.*[15]

There may be a romantic theme that perhaps may be thought unusual for a young Methodist minister. The *Memoir* of Lizzie Mannie Kelley says that her father had proposed marriage to a Miss Sue White and had been rejected. But if David was interested in Miss White, there was another young woman who had an unrequited interest in him. Mary Owen Campbell, a distant cousin, wrote to her father, Governor William B. Campbell, that she had a degree of affection for David. Feelings in the Campbell family were high enough that neither Mary Owen nor her mother went to hear Davis preach his final sermon before leaving for China.[16] In 1869, Mary Owen would become David's second wife.

Following the wedding, David rapidly wrapped up his remaining medical studies and took leave of his friends. His mother accompanied David and Mannie, as the family always called Manerva, to New York City, where they took ship for China. They began their journey on May 6, 1854.[17]

Details about David and Mannie's life in China are sketchy because the correspondence from them to family and friends has not survived, with the exception of one letter and some secondary references to the now-vanished originals. By January 5, 1855, John and Margaret Kelley had received a letter saying their son and daughter-in-law had arrived in Shanghai and were doing well. Another letter arrived just a few days after the first, but then a long pause ensued. Then another letter arrived saying the missionary couple were in good health and fine spirits and were beginning to find "some encouragement at the prospects before them."[18]

The one surviving letter is from Mannie Kelley to Mary Owen Campbell. At the time of writing, Mannie had been away from her family for a year and

The Methodist church at Leeville, where David and his father both preached.

was somewhat discouraged about having been able to accomplish so little. The long ocean voyage had been difficult, and she had spent the time trying to learn something of the language. That learning process was continuing, although David did not allow her to have a teacher since he had decided that the language was too difficult for her to learn. Mannie, however, was picking up some Chinese from the woman who worked as her housemaid and cook.

The young Chinese woman who worked for Mannie had served several missionary couples before the Kelleys and had been learning English for eight years. She had developed a lively interest in Christianity, but she refused to join the church. At an earlier period, she had been employed by Baptist missionaries, and they had convinced her that she would have to be immersed to become a member of their congregation. The young Chinese woman felt she would appear ridiculous standing before a group of people in sopping wet clothes, so she refused to be baptized. The Methodists had not yet convinced her that sprinkling would do just as well as immersion if she chose to join them.

The most important news in the letter was that Mannie and David would soon have a house of their own because a baby was on the way. This child, Mamie Kelley, was born on July 7, 1855.[19]

COMING HOME

The tenure of David and Mannie on the mission field was brief. The reasons for their departure are not fully known but seem to have included Mannie's rather poor health. By late 1855, the couple had decided to return to the United States with their young daughter. By the time they began their trip, Mannie was pregnant a second time. The journey home became a very sad one, enough so to have crushed the spirits of many people. While aboard ship little Mimi, as Mamie was called, died and was buried at sea. Their second child, another daughter, was born after they reached New York City but was very weak. The child died in Richmond, Virginia, and was buried there.[20]

It must have been a brokenhearted couple that returned to Tennessee. David became the pastor of Union Methodist Church near Lebanon for 1856 and the next year was assigned to the Chickasaw Church in Tuscumbia, Alabama. This church was near his wife's family home. In 1858 and 1859, David was pastor of the Methodist church in Franklin, Tennessee.[21]

Quite clearly, the young man who had once preached only on "general topics" was becoming a scholarly and eloquent preacher. He was being assigned to larger churches, and the practice of medicine had been left behind in China.

The year 1860 saw David and Mannie Kelley moving to Huntsville, Alabama. Huntsville was a prosperous town, the seat of Madison County. The town was surrounded by rich soil that produced large crops of cotton. Transportation was provided by the Memphis & Charleston (M&C) Railroad and by a canal that linked the town to the nearby Tennessee River.

Since the Methodist Episcopal Church, South, taught that the church should have nothing to say about political issues, there is no record of what David C. Kelley thought about the growing sectional crisis, nor is there a record of his reaction to Alabama's secession from the Union on January 11, 1861, and the subsequent formation of the Confederate government at Montgomery. Kelley was not a slaveholder; it appears that he and his wife had been given a slave as a wedding present from the bride's parents, but this man had been sold to David's father before the couple left for China and they never again were involved with slaveholding. David's actions would soon reveal what his heart and mind held.

Chapter 2

Outbreak of the War

THE KELLEY TROOPERS

David Kelley had no use for chaplains in military service. He was a man of God, but he was aligned with the "church militant." As a missionary in China he had seen, and associated with, chaplains. These men had not made a favorable impression either by their piety or by the reception they received from the men they were supposed to serve.

Later, Kelley wrote: "My first acquaintance with the chaplains of the army and navy was when I was in the East in the fifties. This acquaintance led me to avoid the chaplaincy in the Confederate army. The chaplain's position needs some more honorable recognition, for neither as officer nor private was he properly recognized. Between the two he was not honored."[1] So Kelley decided he would go to war as a man of war.

Several companies of infantry had already been raised in Huntsville and the surrounding area of Madison County. Kelley felt the cavalry would be a service that would suit him better and that the mounted arm would be well suited to operations in the rural area of the South he knew from lifelong residence. Now that Lincoln had called for troops and the first shots had been fired at Fort Sumter, Kelley felt the need to act. Several groups of cavalry were being formed in the vicinity of Huntsville, including the Pope Walker Troopers, the Madison Cavalry and a group that included members of the First Methodist Church in Huntsville. The pastor was persuaded to accept leadership of this group, and it became known as the Kelley Troopers. Just what his wife thought of this is not recorded, but a daughter born in 1862 said that her mother always was remembered as "a Union woman."

One of the initial enlistees was Frank Gurley, a man who would become well known as a cavalryman under General Nathan Bedford Forrest and as the leader of detached troops opposing U.S. occupation of north Alabama.[2] Because of its central location, Huntsville was declared the training center for these troops. Patriotic citizens took the troopers into their homes, providing room and board, while those who could not be accommodated in private residences were welcomed at the Huntsville Hotel, where they stayed as guests of the house.

David C. Kelley in Confederate uniform. *Courtesy Huntsville/Madison Co. Public Library.*

Among the citizens offering hospitality to the recruits in the Kelley Troopers was Dr. Samuel Maverick Van Wyck, a man with New York ancestry whose father had moved to South Carolina and then to Huntsville. Not anxious to join the army in the first wave of enthusiasm that accompanied secession, Dr. Van Wyck had become associated with a local defense unit. The influence of his pastor at the First Methodist Church, and the inspiration of the volunteer cavalryman he housed, convinced the doctor to leave his wife and four small sons to join the men mustered under David C. Kelley.[3] His story would become intertwined with saving the life of Bedford Forrest.

As novice cavalrymen, Kelley and the other recruits would have studied the *Trooper's Manual*, a textbook adapted by Colonel J. Lucius Davis from the *Poinsett Tactics*, the standard training manual used by the United States from 1841 to 1861. Under these regulations, a regiment consisted of five squadrons, a squadron of two troops or companies, with each company containing eighty men, a captain and two lieutenants.[4] As an educated man,

Kelley would have been a good student and may well have been assisted in his efforts by one of the cadets who had returned to Huntsville from West Point. Because of the small size of the unit, training was limited to learning to form column of fours, go from column into line abreast and basic horse management. In preparation for combat, the men would have to learn to form line by squadron, with successive squadron lines following at intervals of 150 to 200 paces. Weapons were lacking in number and quality, so most of the early training was in formation drill.

In August 1861, after a brief period of training in Huntsville, the Kelley Troopers and the other local units—about eighty men in all, enough for a regulation-size company—loaded their horses on stockcars and took their seats in the passenger cars of the Memphis & Charleston Railroad for a journey to Memphis, the site of Confederate mobilization in west Tennessee.[5] It appears that the young Chinese man Dzau Tsz-zeh, known by the English name of Charles K. Marshall, accompanied Kelley as a personal servant.[6]

Companies were arriving in Memphis from all over the region, and the Confederate authorities there were working feverishly to organize these small groups into larger units and to send them into the field. Among those forming a unit was a former member of the Memphis city council and local businessman, Nathan Bedford Forrest. In July, Forrest had been invited by Tennessee governor Isham Harris to form a battalion for active service. Forrest immediately advertised in the Memphis-area papers and sent representatives all over northern Mississippi and Alabama looking for recruits. The Kelley Rangers were assigned to the battalion to be commanded by Forrest, and when the battalion was organized, David C. Kelley was made the adjutant and promoted to the rank of major. Kelley's mother was distantly related to Forrest's wife, and this family tie may have smoothed the path for having the Alabama troopers included in the command. The position of adjutant demanded careful record keeping and close attention to detail. Probably, Kelley's assignment to this post can be attributed to the skills developed by his education, but Kelley may first have been brought to Forrest's attention by the fact that, through his mother, Kelley was related to the family of Forrest's wife, Mary Montgomery. At any rate, the job of adjutant put Kelley into daily personal contact with Bedford Forrest, and a close bond developed between the men, as evidenced by Forrest presenting to Kelley a pistol engraved "NBF to DCK."

Forrest was noted for his business success and also for his lack of formal education. Often thought of as a man of rough manners and crude speech,

Nathan Bedford Forrest, Kelley's commander and friend. *Courtesy Library of Congress.*

Forrest, in reality, was usually a mild, soft-spoken man with a sense of respect for both education and religion. Forrest had been a Union man and had opposed secession. But the call for troops to invade the South had changed the minds of many men, Kelley and Forrest among them. They shared a belief that they were fighting to defend their homes. Despite being mild-mannered on most occasions, when roused to anger Forrest was fully capable of turning the air blue with profanity and making the object of his wrath regret that he had become the focus of Forrest's ire. With these characteristics, it is not surprising that Forrest liked Kelley and recognized the potential contribution the minister could make to his organization. Kelley, for his part, saw something attractive in Forrest and was willing to overlook the outbursts of anger and bad language in order to have Forrest as a commander, mentor and friend.

The assignment of Alabama troops to regiments commanded by men from other states did not sit well with J. Withers Clay, the editor of the *Huntsville Democrat.* Clay addressed this issue on October 16, 1861, by saying:

*We may add that two companies have gone from Madison to Tennessee—
one, the "Madison Guards," Capt. Hundley, which has been attached to
some Tennessee regiments—the other the "Madison Cavalry," Capt. Kelley,
as an independent company, its destination not being yet fixed, we believe.
We entered our protest at length last week, against the policy of independent
companies leaving Alabama to be attached to regiments or battalions of
other States. Our reasons, were in brief, first, that neither those companies
nor the State of Alabama were likely to receive any credit, or reap any
honor, for any of their heroic deeds or brilliant achievements—that they
will have no place on the historic page, but Tennessee and the Tennessee
regiments to which they are attached will reap all the glory and honor—
secondly, that the departure of independent companies will, in proportion to
their number, diminish the military strength of Alabama and her ability to
respond to future requisitions of troops.[7]*

By early October, the Kelley Troopers had become Company F, Forrest's
Cavalry Battalion. Serving with the Huntsville men were troopers from
Kentucky, southern Alabama, Texas, north Alabama and many from the
Memphis area of Tennessee.[8] The complaints of the Huntsville newspapers
did not bother Kelley and the men who were busy training; they seemed
quite happy with their lot. Early in October, Kelley had written to the
Huntsville Democrat:

Camp Forest, Near Memphis
*Editor, Democrat: To satisfy the inquiries of many of our Madison friends,
please say to them, that our Troop is pleasantly located three miles from
Memphis, and that the Government has meted out to us ample supplies, in
arms, forage, and provisions. We have equipment for twelve men, who were
on our roll but have not yet reached our camp. I expect to be in Huntsville
the 9th or 10th of October, and will bring down with me any recruits who
may wish to come with me. We have four horses, which we will supply to
good men, and will procure shot guns. All clothing and other equipment we
have from the Government.[9]*

There is no record of Kelley's visit to Huntsville or his success in recruiting
additional men. However, when the battalion was formally organized under
Forrest, Company F carried eighty men plus officers on its roll. With the
organization of the battalion, Kelley was elected major and the command of
the company passed to Joseph B. Hambrick.[10] This battalion, which would

evolve into the 3rd Tennessee Cavalry, would forever be known as Forrest's Old Regiment, and the name of David C. Kelley would remain associated with the unit.

During the training period, Forrest left Kelley in command of the unit and made a trip to Louisville to secure arms for his command. Using his business connections, Forrest purchased several hundred Colt revolvers and Maynard rifles, which he successfully smuggled back to Tennessee. The Maynard was a favorite with cavalrymen who could get them. Patented in 1856 by Dr. Edward Maynard and manufactured in Chickopee, Massachusetts, the Maynard used a metal .52 cartridge. In order to load the weapon, the soldier pulled down the trigger guard, which caused the hinged barrel to tip forward. The brass cartridge was then inserted into the chamber, and then the trigger guard was swung back to close the breech. The weapon was detonated by either of two means; a traditional percussion cap could be placed on the nipple or a roll of paper caps could be inserted. These paper caps were much like the rolls used in children's cap pistols. The problem for Confederates would be replacing the brass cartridges. Southern soldiers learned to pick up their spent cartridge casings and save them for reloading.

Because the battalion was made up of men from so many different areas of the Confederacy, the election of Kelley as major illustrates some interesting points. Had the unit come from a single geographic location, it would have been expected that a man of local reputation or standing would have been elected to this important post; however, the diverse place of origin of the companies that made up the unit, along with the brief time the men had been together, suggest that Kelley had a charismatic personality and possessed some ability as an organizer and leader of men. This supposition is supported by the success Kelley would have throughout his military career in securing the cheerful obedience of those who came under his command.

By the second week of October 1861, the battalion was ordered into the field at Fort Donelson. Kelley led a group of one hundred men from the training grounds near Memphis to Nashville, arriving on October 21. On that day he drew forage for one hundred horses for seven days, a total of seven hundred rations or 8,400 pounds of corn. Kelley signed the proper requisition form asserting he had not been foraging during any of the time he was asking for rations and also swore he had received the full ration of corn from Major G.W. Cunningham of the Quartermaster Department.[11]

In the Field with Forrest

The entire battalion reassembled at Fort Donelson, or Dover, by the end of October and began to carry out routine duties of patrolling, an activity that would have the positive effect of familiarizing the men with an area where they would win fame in February 1862. As construction progressed on Fort Donelson on the Cumberland River and nearby Fort Henry on the Tennessee River, the Confederates were concerned about the presence of a new weapon: the ironclad gunboats being built by the United States Navy, some of which were already probing down the Tennessee and up the Cumberland. No such weapon of war had been seen before in this country, and no one knew just what its potential might be.

When a Union gunboat, the USS *Conestoga*, reached Port Tobacco on the Cumberland, Forrest's battalion was ordered to move downstream to keep an eye on the intruder. This order was countermanded by General Lloyd Tilghman, who told Forrest to come to his headquarters at Hopkinsville, Kentucky. From there, the command was sent to the Ohio River to watch the stretch of river between the mouth of the Cumberland and the mouth of the Green River. Kelley was sent in independent command of a squadron to intercept a transport carrying supplies for the U.S. Army.

Moving to Princeton, Kentucky, Kelley placed his men in ambush along the banks of the river and waited until the steamboat came into sight. Allowing it to come even with his position, the major ordered his men to open fire on the pilothouse. After a few rounds had peppered the boat, Kelley stepped into the open and yelled for the pilot to put the boat alongside the bank or Kelley would open fire with his artillery—a weapon that was conspicuous by its absence. The boat, however, did not want to risk the presence of cannon and pulled ashore. Will Corder, one of the men with Kelley, recalled in 1922 that "that thing was loaded with things we needed, things like sugar, coffee, blankets, and even some rifles."[12] The *Conestoga* was still on the prowl on the Cumberland and had moved up that stream to the vicinity of Canton, Kentucky, with the intention of seizing clothes stored there by the Confederates. Warned by a friendly citizen of Smithland that the gunboat was making this move, Forrest recalled Kelley and moved the entire battalion to Canton. This time artillery was present, a four-pounder gun commanded by Lieutenant Sullivan.

Utilizing the experience gained by Kelley, the cavalrymen took cover in ravines along the riverbanks, and the gun was placed in a "masked," or camouflaged, position. The *Conestoga* cautiously approached the landing but then dropped back and opened its gun ports. Immediately, the Confederate cannon opened fire, but much more effective was the rifle fire from the dismounted men. Will Corder describes this fight:

> Our whole battalion rode about 30 miles to fight the thing. We didn't have any artillery except one little four pounder. We hid it in the trees at the bend of the river and waited for the boat. We blew into it and did some damage. The gunboat backed off and opened its gun ports. It had armor and about eight heavy guns. They blew up a lot of dirt, but we were hid in some ravines. We used our Maynard rifles and started pickin' off those sailors right out of those open gun ports. We fought that thing for seven or eight hours, and it withdrew. We learned we didn't have to be afeared of them things. We lost but five or six men and they lost twenty five or so.[13]

Among those who were recognized for the accuracy of their fire were two men who had come to the command as part of the Kelley Rangers: Private R.H. Balch, who would one day rise to command many of the man engaged at Princeton; and Dr. Van Wyck, who had been personally recruited by Kelley.[14]

The USS *Conestoga* had been built in Brownsville, Pennsylvania, in 1859 as a riverboat. It was purchased by the United States Army in June 1861, converted to a timberclad gunboat and placed under the command of Lieutenant Seth Ledyard Phelps, United States Navy. *Conestoga* was armed with six thirty-two-pounder smoothbores. Phelps took a different view of the engagement at Canton, saying that he had been warned by a civilian that an ambush had been laid for him and that the Confederates opened fire at a range of fifty yards. He returned fire with canister from his big guns only to have his boat peppered with rifle fire. The only casualty Phelps admitted was a flesh wound inflicted on his pet dog, Sancho.[15]

As soon as *Conestoga* departed, the cavalrymen mounted up and returned to their base at Hopkinsville, Kentucky. There two additional companies, commanded by Captains Charles McDonald and D.D. Davis, joined the command, raising their numbers to regimental strength. Although winter had arrived, Forrest soon grew restless in camp and requested permission to make a reconnaissance to the banks of the Ohio to determine the intentions of General T.L. Crittenden and his Union force. Kelley helped lead the 450 chosen men on this scout, spending twelve days in the open. Already the men who "rode with Forrest" had gained confidence in his leadership, as Kelley reflected in later times:

The command found that it was Forrest's single will, impervious to argument, appeal, or threat, which was ever to be the governing impulse in their movements. Every thing necessary to supply their wants, to make them comfortable, he was quick to do, save to change his plans, to which everything had to bend. New men naturally grumbled, and were dissatisfied in the execution, but, when the work was achieved, were soon reconciled by the pride they felt in the achievement.[16]

It was while on this expedition that Kelley lost his friend and neighbor, Dr. Samuel M. Van Wyck. Near the village of Marion, Kentucky, Kelley was with Forrest when news was brought of the arrest of a prominent citizen who was pro-Confederate. Forrest decided to arrest the Unionist neighbor who had caused the arrest. With Kelley and Van Wyck in tow, Forrest led a detachment to the house of the informer. As the group rode up the lane to the house, a shot was fired from the doorway. Dr. Van Wyck, who was wearing a full Confederate uniform, was hit and killed instantly. The assailant made his escape, apparently having thought he was firing at the commanding officer of the unit.[17] This death of a man he had personally recruited was a shock to Kelley, and he dealt with the loss by personally conducting the funeral for his friend.

Returning to Hopkinsville, Kelley wrote a report of the expedition and then took part in settling the command into winter quarters, a state they were not to enjoy for very long. On December 26, Forrest, assisted by Kelley, led three hundred men out of camp to keep an eye on a reported Federal move. On December 28, near the village of Sacramento, Kentucky, the forces met. Forrest had come on the field in a hurry after marching rapidly for several miles. Kelley had taken a slower pace and had kept his three companies, E, F and G, in a compact unit. At the initial meeting, the Yankees were uncertain if they were seeing hostile or friendly troops, but Forrest soon settled the issue by taking a Maynard rifle from one of his men and firing the first shot.

About that time, Kelley came up with his men, and Forrest hurriedly laid out a plan. Kelley had kept his men under tight control and had maintained formation, thinking it better to arrive on the field as a compact unit as opposed to a loose group of individuals. A number of men were dismounted and placed in the center of the line with instructions to keep up a lively fire on the Union position. Captain J.W. Starnes had recently joined Forrest, and he was ordered to take thirty men and move to the Union left, while Kelley was to take sixty men and move to the Union right. As these two flanking columns emerged from cover, moving toward their objectives, the Union line wavered. Immediately, Forrest ordered the charge, and every Confederate who could get on a horse went forward. The Union retreat swept through Sacramento, and a running fight continued for several miles beyond and ended with Forrest in a fight for his life, contending with four Union soldiers. Forrest killed one, a second was thrown from his horse as Forrest crashed his mount into him and the others ran as Kelley came up with reinforcements. Kelley later remembered vividly what he saw: "His face had flushed until it bore a striking resemblance to a painted Indian warrior, and his eyes, usually so mild in their expression, flashed with the intense glare of the panther about to spring on its prey. In fact, he looked as little like the Forrest of our mess-table as the storms of December resembles the quiet of June."[18]

One of the soldiers at Sacramento, Captain J.C. Blanton, commander of Company C, remembered:

> *By that evening we were convinced that Forrest and Kelley were wise selections for our leaders. And in all the battles that followed in which these two men were actors, they well sustained the reputation made on the field of Sacramento.*
>
> *Kelley's motto was "In the path of duty there is no danger and the duty of a soldier is to obey orders." Forrest made the path of duty plain and Kelley walked in it.*[19]

One interesting sidelight on the engagement at Sacramento was the appearance on the field of Miss Molly Morehead, a resident of the village. She made her way out to Confederate lines to tell Forrest that the troops there were indeed Union men. Forrest's official report says:

> *Her untied tresses, floating in the breeze, infused nerve into my arm and kindled knightly chivalry in my heart. These words were actually written by Kelley but reflect what Forrest wanted to say. Kelley said though indisposed to the use of the pen himself, he had clear and exact ideas of what he wanted written, and few were more exacting in requiring a precise statement of the ideas furnished.*[20]

It seems as though "that devil Forrest" and his preacher were both capable of uttering the romantic platitudes prevalent in nineteenth-century culture.

Kelley and the rest of Forrest's men returned to Hopkinsville and spent the next weeks based there. Kelley had decided that education in military matters was important and spent time reading training manuals and then applying these lessons in drilling the men. Some who are not well informed as to the nature of Forrest's command persist in calling it "undisciplined." Others attribute to Forrest and his officers a lack of education. Both these assertions are contradicted by the evidence. In his careers as plantation owner and businessman, Forrest had long since learned the necessity of discipline in order to achieve objectives. Kelley, and the other field and line officers in the command, were men who possessed a level of formal education, all of them more than did Forrest. These men used their education to help Forrest achieve the high standards of training and discipline necessary to form an effective fighting force. Operating, as they often did, in detached and exposed positions, the command would not have survived without a superior level of training and discipline. Outpost duty and scouting made for a varied routine, but in early February, orders came to return to an area already visited once, the vicinity of Fort Donelson.

FORT DONELSON: THE FIRST REAL BATTLE

Forrest's command arrived at Fort Donelson on February 10. Kelley settled the men into bivouac as Forrest sought out the commanding officer to receive his orders. As Kelley carried out this routing duty, he could hardly have imagined that before a week had passed the man he followed and the men he helped lead would have established a legendary reputation. It is clear that Kelley had already won the trust of Forrest. Kelley's success in independent command in the incident involving the transport boat, his conduct under fire in the confrontation with *Conestoga* and his boldness in leading one of the flank attacks at Sacramento had proved to Forrest that the young Methodist minister was a man of war as well as a man of God. The trust Forrest placed in Kelley would that week become a personal bond that would outlast the war.

Early on February 11, Kelley was ordered to take three companies and move toward Fort Henry, now in Union hands, along the Ridge Road. There were two roads providing direct access between Forts Henry and Donelson, Ridge Road to the south and Telegraph Road to the north. Both of them had been cut during 1861 by Confederates constructing the two posts. While the trees and other obstructions had been cleared, these "roads" were really dirt trails that traversed steep ridges and deep hollows. At the bottom of most of the hollows were small streams whose course was marked by mud thanks to recent rains. As Kelley moved toward Fort Henry, blue-clad infantry was moving toward him preceded by four companies of cavalry. General U.S. Grant ordered General

John McClernand to move his division some five and a half miles out the Ridge Road as part of the Union advance on Fort Donelson. About three miles out from Fort Donelson, the Confederate troopers met the Yanks and drove them back some six miles, taking a prisoner and wounding several.[21] On February 12, the Confederate cavalry engaged the Union infantry more strongly. Again ordered out to scout the U.S. advance, Forrest encountered their cavalry about two miles from Fort Donelson. This time he sent in his advance guard supported by three dismounted companies. This stand forced the commander of the Union's leading brigade, Colonel Richard Oglesby, to deploy his men and attack the ridge where the Confederates were posted. Thinking he was opposed by infantry, Oglesby shifted to his right toward the Pinery Road looking for an alternate route toward Fort Donelson; Forrest shifted with him. Coming into a new position, Forrest attacked as soon as the leading Union cavalry came into sight and was soon hotly engaged. Since he was under orders not to bring on a general engagement, Forrest looked for a way to disengage his men. Kelley offered to charge the Union lines with three companies under his command in order to create a situation in which the advance guard could withdraw. With the full approval of Forrest, the attack was made, and Kelley not only drove off the Union cavalry but briefly engaged their infantry and artillery as well. At this point, about 2:00 p.m., Forrest received orders to withdraw his men into the Confederate lines. Forrest, ably assisted by David Kelley, had delayed the Union advance for five hours.[22] During the day, some of the cavalrymen had fought as infantry; that night they all worked as sappers, digging trenches. Other than the "Water Battery" facing the Cumberland River, Fort Donelson was in an incomplete state.

The work on the trenches and breastworks was completed none too soon because before daylight on February 13, Union skirmishers were probing toward the Confederate lines. For most of the day, while three strong attacks probed the Southern lines and surrounded the fortifications, Forrest and his command were uninvolved; the fighting in the trenches was no place for cavalry. As the day wore on, however, someone felt that the fierce spirit displayed by Forrest's men was needed to counteract the sniping of Birge's sharpshooters, men specially chosen and trained for their work and armed with sporting rifles. Forrest and Kelley led a select detachment of Confederates to the front lines to spot and shoot Birge's men, and after some two hours, the sniping had been damped down. During this time, while visiting Porter's Battery where Birge's snipers were especially troublesome, Forrest had taken a rifle from one of his men and picked off one of the Yankee riflemen. A subordinate officer in Porter's Battery was Lieutenant John Morton. Before

Porter's Battery at Fort Donelson, where Forrest and Kelley met John Morton.
Courtesy John Walsh, Dover Relics.

the end of 1862, Morton would have begun an association with Forrest and Kelley that would last as long as any of the men lived. Darkness stopped the fight but also brought an unwelcome change of weather with biting wind, sleet and freezing temperatures.

Friday, February 14, was anxiously awaited by men on both sides of the line. For Kelley, the day brought the prospect of only limited action as infantrymen on both sides tried to solidify their positions. The unanswered question was "What would the Union navy do?" The smoke from the stacks of the ironclad gunboats could be seen downriver where the boats were anchored around a bend, sheltered from cannon fire from the fort. About the middle of the afternoon, the boats moved upriver against the batteries of Fort Donelson, the armored *St. Louis*, *Louisville*, *Pittsburg* and *Carondelet* leading with the timberclads *Conestoga* and *Tyler* some four hundred yards behind them.[23] Heavy artillery on both sides was soon booming, and the outcome was awaited with anxiety on all sides. Except, perhaps, by D.C. Kelley.

The bivouac of Forrest's cavalry was in a ravine, out of the line of fire. A member of the regiment, Captain J.C. Blanton of Company C, noted:

> *During this bombardment and when it looked like the furies of hell were turned loose on us, I looked down the line and saw Kelley sitting on a camp stool leaning against a tent pole reading his Bible. My curiosity was at once*

*excited, and wondering if it were possible for a man to be interested even in
reading God's word under such circumstances, I walked to where he was,
stood close to him until I was satisfied that he was deeply interested in the
Book. I went back and called some comrades' attention to it, and after going
close to him they returned in perfect amazement that any man could be so
composed amid such roaring of cannon shots, and screaming shells. Why,
the very earth was quivering under us.* [24]

Forrest did not appear to share the composure of his adjutant. At some
point in the afternoon, Forrest approached Kelley, and the two watched the
battering the fort was taking. Suddenly Forrest exclaimed, "Parson, for God's
sake pray! Nothing but God Almighty can save that fort!" [25]

This appeal to divine intervention may sound surprising to those who
have only a passing knowledge of Forrest and who know of his propensity
to vulgar language in times of excitement, but the request for prayer was no
surprise to Kelley. Since the very beginning of their association, Kelley had
functioned as an unofficial chaplain for the headquarters staff and, indeed,
for the entire regiment. Like many men who grew up on the ragged edge
of the developing frontier, Forrest had great respect for religion even though
formal affiliation with a church was often neglected. Forrest did not formally

The river battery at Fort Donelson—"Parson, for God's sake pray! Nothing but
God Almighty can save that fort!" *Courtesy John Walsh, Donelson Relics.*

join a church until near the end of his life, when he became a communicant of the Cumberland Presbyterian Church in Memphis.

Dr. J.B. Cowan was Forrest's personal physician, as well as chief surgeon for the command during almost the entire war. Cowan noted: "We never started on an expedition but what the men were drawn up in line and the chaplain, while the heads of all were uncovered, evoked God's blessing on our cause. Nothing called down Forrest's quicker or brought on surer punishment than for a man to disturb religious service in any part of the camp."[26]

The excitement shown here by Forrest is rather unusual. Forrest already had experience with gunboats and had been under fire from the *Conestoga* several weeks earlier. Perhaps the difference was that the attack on the fort was being made by ironclads instead of timberclads, or perhaps the issue was the large number of guns being fired. At any rate, the Union attack failed, and the gunboats fell back down the river to seek cover around a bend in the stream.

During the night, a call went out for all officers to assemble at headquarters. Forrest left Kelley with the regiment and attended the meeting. The goals of the Confederate command structure were somewhat confused, but a consensus seems to have been reached that because the main army under General Albert Sidney Johnston had made its retreat from Bowling Green to Nashville, the task of the garrison at Fort Pillow had been completed; they had bought time for the forces in Kentucky to fall back to the south side of the Cumberland River. That being the case, it was now appropriate for the Fort Donelson troops to break out and abandon their position. That was to be the task for Saturday, February 15.

Forrest had been described as a "panther" by some of his men. On this Saturday, he would indeed be like a panther on the hunt because Forrest would lead his command all across the field, mauling everything in his path. As second in command, Kelley would be in the thick of the action, usually in charge of one wing of the regiment while Forrest commanded from a post in the center of the line. The general concept Forrest would follow was to attack at every opportunity and to place himself in the hottest part of the action. From that position, in the thick of the fight, Forrest felt he could sense the direction the fight was taking and could best control the action.[27] Kelley seems to have shared this point of view and acted in keeping with it himself. This shared philosophy of action helps explain the bond of trust that existed between Forrest and Kelley.

As day was breaking, around 6:00 a.m., Forrest's command led the Confederate assault column out of the fortifications using a country lane some two hundred yards to the left of the extreme flank of their trenches.

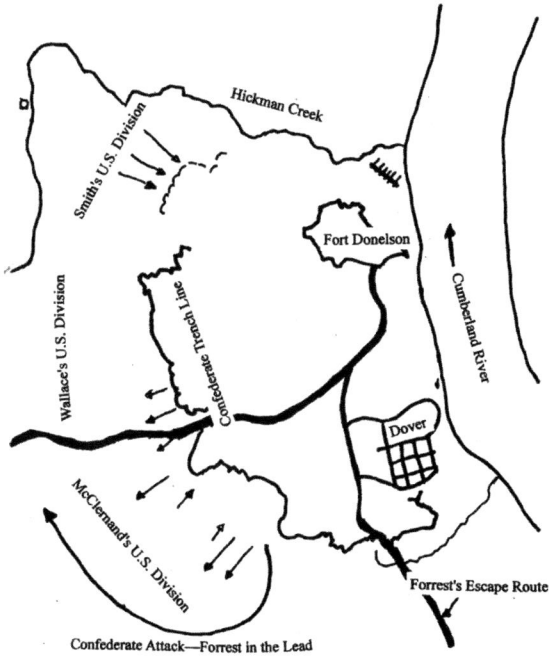

Confederate Attack—Forrest in the Lead

FORT DONELSON

Second day of fighting at Fort Donelson. Forrest and Kelley help open an escape route. *Map by Martha Bradley.*

According to his report, Forrest found the enemy alert and ready, and he engaged them until the infantry could come up. Once the foot troops were in place, Forrest took his men to the left of the line and began attempting to turn the opposing flank of the Union line.[28] This proved to be a slow and costly process. The blue-clad troops facing the Confederates were commanded by John McArthur, and they were well placed on Dudley's Hill. Unremitting pressure finally began to tell, and by 9:00 a.m., these men were finding their right flank and rear threatened by Forrest's move.

As Forrest led the move against the Union infantry, Kelley was assigned the task of keeping an eye on the Northern cavalry who were in position to protect the Union flank. Although there were four regiments with men present—2nd and 4th U.S. Regulars and 2nd and 4th Illinois Volunteers— the opposing horsemen acted merely as spectators and took no part in the daylong fighting. Kelley and Forrest were defying the conventional wisdom that cavalry could not take on infantry in an open field fight. The men under their command were constantly moving forward both on horse and on foot, probing both the front and the flanks of the opposing infantry. When signs of confusion or retreat were seen in the U.S. lines, both men were quick to order an attack to exploit the situation.

Finally, the Union line had been driven back for about a mile, uncovering the Forge Road, the line the Confederates could use to retreat toward Nashville and stay clear of the backwater from the flooded Cumberland River. As the troops of McArthur fell back, resistance continued to be offered by Battery E of the 2nd Illinois Light Artillery commanded by Captain Adolph Swartz. Forrest sent Kelley toward one flank of this battery and took the rest of the men toward the other flank. The charging horsemen overran the guns, capturing three of the pieces and forcing the others back.[29] As the U.S. forces fell back to make another stand on another ridge, the 11th Illinois and 31st Illinois Infantry temporarily checked the Confederates. Forrest took a look at this line and sent Kelley around the Union right flank while Forrest approached from the front. As Kelley's men gained the rear of the Illinois position, the unit collapsed and ran off the field, closely pursued by the gray cavalry.[30] This is an unusually clear example of cavalry successfully attacking infantry. The success of Kelley's attack can be attributed to the speed with which the horsemen closed on the infantry and to the fact that the Confederates were armed with Maynard and Sharps rifles, giving them the firepower to take on infantry.

The Union forces made another stand on the Wynns Ferry Road, but their line had a right-angle bend that allowed the Confederates to enfilade the bend with both rifle and artillery fire. The U.S. position was anchored by Battery B, 1st Illinois Light Artillery, commanded by Captain Edward McAllister. This battery was made up of twenty-four-pounder smoothbore howitzers. In response to a request from General Gideon Pillow, Forrest moved his men to attack this stronghold. The regiment was formed in column of squadrons that charged in succession up the ravine in which the battery was posted. Each squadron deployed one company to the left and right while in motion, reached a convenient distance and fired a volley to be succeeded by the next squadron. This technique had been followed twice without success when the 2nd Kentucky Infantry, CS, came on the scene. Following a quick conference, it was decided that the cavalry would strike for the flanks of the battery position while the infantry came straight in to challenge the support troops, braving the fire of the cannon as they came.

This attack struck just as McAllister ran out of ammunition. This time, a Union stampede occurred, and the horsemen had the best of the encounter while the 2nd Kentucky came up as fast as they could to join the fun. Forrest lost his horse in this attack, the animal going down with seven wounds, while the lieutenant colonel took fifteen holes in his overcoat. Forrest dismounted a trooper in order to secure another horse, but this animal soon was down, and Forrest left Kelley in command of making a reconnaissance down the Wynns Ferry Road.[31] Again, the cavalry, led by Forrest and Kelley, had done something horse soldiers were not thought capable of doing—they had successfully attacked infantry supported by artillery and had broken the enemy line.

It was now about 2:30 p.m. The Union line had been folded back, but a counterattack was about to be launched from the left of the Northern lines. General Grant had been absent from the field during the morning, attending a conference with the naval commanders. When he returned to find the right wing of his army in retreat, Grant decided the Confederates opposite his left must be few in number. Attacking there brought a limited gain of ground but added to the confusion in the ranks of the Confederate high command. Soon an order was given for the gray infantry to retire to their trenches. As they receded, the blue ranks advanced. Kelley kept the field with the cavalry to slow this reoccupation of the ground won with so much blood that morning. By dusk, the only remaining Confederate advantage was the possession of some five thousand rifles gleaned from the field by the men under Kelley's supervision.[32]

During the night of February 15–16, Forrest was again summoned to headquarters. There he was confronted with the astounding news that the fort was to be surrendered. Not pleased with this decision, Forrest announced his plan to leave the fort with his command and any others who chose to go with him. The generals gave their blessing to this proposal, and Forrest left to make good on his proposal.

Just after 4:00 a.m., Forrest led his men out of their bivouac to follow the same road they had taken the day before when they initiated the Confederate attack on the Union flank. A turnoff from this road would take his men across Lick Creek on a locally known ford. Some five hundred men of his own command made up this column with a collection of men from various commands estimated in number from two hundred to one thousand. The men had moved only a few hundred yards when their advance guard reported that the road ahead was blocked. Not believing the report to be true, Forrest and his younger brother, Jeffrey, went ahead

Dover Inn or Surrender House, where Forrest and Kelley refused to surrender.
Courtesy John Walsh, Dover Relics.

themselves to see. Before going on this scout, Forrest placed Kelley in command of the column, telling him that if he (Forrest) was killed then Kelley was to take the men out over the route they had decided on. This is a telling comment since it shows that Kelley was just as determined a man as Forrest was. The two had "drunk from the same canteen." As Forrest suspected, the road was open. The two Forrest brothers rode up onto the hill where so much fighting had taken place the day before and found only wounded Federals. Returning to cross Lick Creek, Forrest marched his command to a point where a second road forked toward Cumberland Iron Works. Leaving Kelley there with a rearguard, the rest of the escaped Confederates continued their cold march toward the next battle.[33]

NASHVILLE TO SHILOH

Forrest's command covered about twenty-five miles that day before stopping near Charlotte in Dixon County. The next morning, Forrest led his men into town, but before entering the place the command was given for every man to fire his rifle and reload just in case there were unfriendly troops waiting for them. The only troops in Charlotte were a regiment of Confederate cavalry, but they were nervous over the news that had reached them of the surrender of Fort Donelson. When the unseen men of Forrest's command fired off their rifles, the Confederates in town abandoned their camp and left for Nashville at a rapid rate. Kelley led a detachment into the abandoned camp and ruled that what had been left behind was "spoils of war." By the time the regiment left for Nashville, the men were as well equipped as they had been on arriving at Fort Donelson.[34]

Nightfall found the men some eighteen miles west of Nashville, and the next day the men entered the anxious capital of Tennessee, where some elements of the civilian population were becoming unruly as the Confederate and state authorities began to leave the place. General John B. Floyd had been left in charge of the city, and he assigned to Forrest the duty of acting as provost marshal to control the population and to supervise the evacuation of military supplies. Forrest showed a great deal of proficiency in his assignment. The sites at which disorder were evident were at the warehouses of the commissary and quartermaster departments, where word had been spread that citizens would be allowed to help themselves to stores. Naturally, a crush of unruly people had gathered, but Forrest and his men quickly put an end to the specter of wholesale looting. In reality, the number of people attempting to pillage the military stores was small. Most citizens of Nashville cooperated with the effort to evacuate the supplies, with many men bringing their wagons and teams to the warehouses to assist Forrest in moving the material to the rail yards. Forrest, ably aided by Kelley, moved not only supplies but also sick and wounded men from the hospitals and stripped much valuable machinery from arms manufacturing plants in the town.[35] Even after Union soldiers arrived on the north bank of the Cumberland River, Forrest kept his men at work for another forty-eight hours, ably assisted by David Kelley, "his second in command,…both a willing and capable soldier, quick and studious in the acquisition of military knowledge, as also of the highest courage."[36]

When Forrest's command did ride out of Nashville along the Murfreesboro Pike, it was Kelley who took his now-accustomed place as commander of the rear guard. This time there was not much excitement or tension in the responsibility. The Union troops had plenty to do in occupying Nashville and made no attempt at pursuit. There were short pauses at Murfreesboro, Shelbyville and Fayetteville as the men approached the Tennessee state line. During a pause just south of Murfreesboro, Kelley had a short visit from his father, who told him that Mannie, Kelley's wife, was in Murfreesboro. The

FROM DOVER TO SHILOH

After Fort Donelson, Confederate forces fell back to Corinth and concentrated for Shiloh. *Map by Martha Bradley.*

press of military duties did not allow Kelley to return to town to see her, and the command soon moved on. Kelley, and many of those who rode with him, must have felt a mixture of strong emotions as they traveled from Fayetteville, Tennessee, to Huntsville, Alabama. For many, this was their home, which they had left many weeks before as raw recruits. Now they returned as veterans, but their pleasure at returning home was surely tempered by the knowledge that they could not hold their homes against the enemy who soon would advance from Nashville. One welcome piece of news did come their way on February 23. Forrest announced that he would give his men two weeks' furlough to return to their homes and refit themselves with clothes and, if needed, fresh horses. They were to reassemble on March 10.

While this might seem to be an enormous risk, disbanding a command that had just participated in a failed campaign that allowed the enemy to advance scores of miles into Confederate territory, Forrest was confident that his men were strong in their commitment to the cause of independence. He was not disappointed. On the appointed day, Kelley led back into camp a full complement of men from the area, and the other officers did the same. Every man who had gone on furlough had returned, and many brought recruits with them.[37]

Precisely what David Kelley did during these two weeks is not known. Since he had been pastor of the Methodist church in Huntsville, it is certain that he had many friends there, and it is quite likely that he was invited to fill the pulpit during this brief stay. Certainly, the dashing Reverend Major Kelley would have been sought after for news about the military situation as well as for spiritual comfort. It is not known if Kelley's family was in Huntsville at this time. Kelley and his wife, Manerva, had two children at this time: a daughter, Daisy, born in 1858, and a son, John Harris, born in 1860. Manerva was expecting their third child, who would be another daughter, Elizabeth, born in September 1862. It may be that Manerva Kelley and the children had returned to her family home in Wilson County, Tennessee, when Kelley left Huntsville in 1861.[38]

On March 10, 1862, the reassembled force was ordered to leave Huntsville for Iuka, Mississippi. They reached there on March 16 and were ordered to move seven miles to Burnsville, Mississippi, a station on the Memphis & Charleston Railroad. Additional men joined Forrest at that place, and with ten companies present, the command was formally organized into a regiment. In the subsequent reorganization, Forrest retained his post as colonel but Kelley was selected as lieutenant colonel. The post of major went to R.M. Balch, a former private in the Kelley Troopers who would later have independent command of a battalion of the men now being assembled. In less than a year, David C. Kelley had gone from being a pastor of a Methodist church in a county seat town in north Alabama to being second in command of a cavalry regiment led by a man who was already a legend in the western Confederacy. He had gone from being a man of God to also being a man of war, a seasoned veteran of combat and a man trusted to lead troops in dangerous conditions.

Until March 26, the regiment led by Forrest and Kelley engaged in drill and training. Both Kelley and Forrest were firm believers in the need for discipline and drill to turn men into soldiers. Though many of the men they commanded were veterans, many others were new recruits, and a large part of the unit had been recently added. Training exercises were necessary to create unit cohesion and to teach the new men how to work efficiently with the more experienced troopers. The spirits of Kelley and his original command were dampened by the news that U.S. troops under General Ormsby Mitchell had occupied Huntsville; the church where Kelley had preached now had its basement used as a stable while men bivouacked in the sanctuary. This news, while discouraging, did make them grimly determined to drive the invaders from Dixie. It was while in this mood that orders reached the command on April 3 to take the road for a place

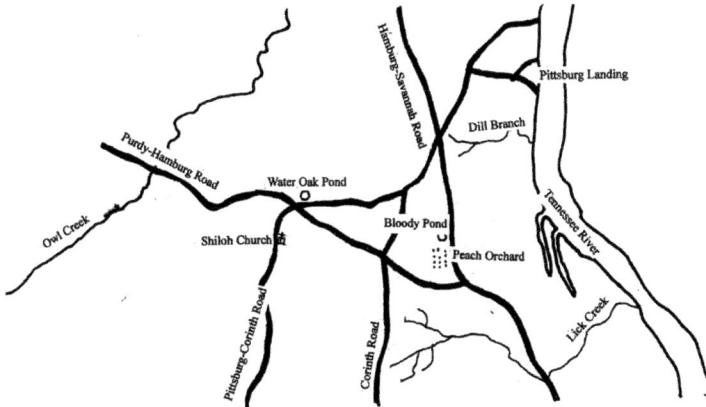

THE FIELD OF SHILOH

The field of Shiloh. *Map by Martha Bradley.*

called Pittsburg Landing on the Tennessee River where Union troops were concentrating. Many of them were camped around a little Methodist church called Shiloh—ironically, a Hebrew word meaning "the place of peace."

Forrest and Kelley led the column as the horsemen screened the advance of the three brigades of infantry commanded by General John C. Breckenridge as the force moved from Burnsville toward Monterrey, Tennessee. What was planned as a swift march leading to an attack on April 5 turned into a slow wallow through seas of mud so that the cavalry outdistanced the foot soldiers. Arriving at Monterrey, Forrest and Kelley were sent forward to a watercourse called Lick Creek to picket the roads leading from the Union positions. On the afternoon of April 5, the regiment was engaged less than two miles from Shiloh Church.

When the battle opened the next morning with a Confederate attack, Forrest and Kelley held their men along Lick Creek to guard a road leading to a landing on the Tennessee River in case the U.S. forces attempted to land men there and turn the right flank of the Confederates. When it was clear this would not occur, the regiment was ordered into the heat of battle and soon found itself in support of the infantry division of General Frank Cheatham. Seeing a Union line of battle consisting of infantry and two batteries, Forrest asked for orders to attack. Cheatham replied that he did not have the authority to give such orders, so Forrest led a charge on the artillery. Making such an attack in wooded and marshy terrain led to a repulse. Later

Lick Creek, on the approach to Shiloh. A restless Forrest left Kelley in command here while he rode to find a place to join the fighting.

in the war, Forrest would not have tried such an attack, but the Napoleonic tradition of cavalry charging artillery was still unchallenged by experience. When the men reassembled following the attack, Forrest turned to Kelley and commented, "Well, parson, no need to talk about the 'best way' to attack a battery; truth is they ain't even no 'good' way, never mind a 'best' way." A little later, Cheatham's infantry swept forward with Forrest guarding their flanks, and this assault forced back the Union defenders, weakening the position in the tangle of woods and along a sunken road that was acquiring the name by which it is still known—"the Hornets' nest." When the Confederates finally overran the position following a massive artillery bombardment, Kelley was ordered by Forrest to provide an escort for the 2,200 Union infantry who had surrendered in the "nest." Obeying this order, Kelley escorted the dejected Yankees to the rear until he found the Confederate provost. Relieved of the prisoners, Kelley was returning to his post when, as he later recalled:

> We came in sight of a long line of Confederate infantry forming at the base of a not very elevated ridge. Leaving a group of officers sitting their horses just in rear of this line, a staff officer galloped to the head of our

column, saluted, and said, "General Bragg's compliments, and requests to know what cavalry this is?" The reply was given "Forrest's Regiment," when the officer added: "Gen. Bragg requests that you place your command in position to attack the battery on the hill in flank when he moves to the attack in front." Leaving my command at the foot of the ridge, I rode to the top to get full knowledge of the ground over which the charge would have to be made. While making my observations, two guns from the battery moved rapidly to the rear; the others were deserted, and there was not left on the field a single Federal gun in action. The gunboats were firing, but the balls were passing high over our heads through the tree tops; the banks of the river did not allow their depression.

Returning to my command I conveyed to one of Gen. Bragg's staff the results of my observations, adding; "The whole Federal army in sight is in utter disorder, and will surrender in five minutes after your line of infantry appears on the top of the ridge." He replied: "Gen. Bragg will be on the top of the ridge in five minutes." Not more than five minutes had passed when the whole line of infantry extending to my right farther than the eye could reach threw down their arms and lay at east on the ground. When I sought the meaning of this sudden change, and officer of Gen. Bragg's staff said to me: "Gen. Bragg has just received an order from Gen. Beauregard to move his command from under the fire of the gunboats and bivouac for the night," adding, "Gen. Bragg is foaming at the mouth like a mad tiger." After reading many accounts of the battle of Shiloh, my conviction now is what it was at the time: had Gen. Bragg not received this order, the Federal army would have surrendered on the afternoon of the first day's fight. Gunboat shells may have been falling at the rear where Gen. Beauregard was; they were passing harmlessly over the heads of our men at the front, and not a Federal land battery was in action.[39]

Many contend that what Kelley witnessed was the decisive decision of the day, as the relaxation of pressure on the U.S. forces by the Confederates allowed Grant the time and space he needed to receive reinforcements from Don Carlos Buell during the night.

On April 7, the Confederates were forced back to the vicinity of Shiloh Church and, from there, took up the march back to Corinth. Kelley saw considerable action during this second day of fighting since Forrest's regiment provided flank protection for Breckenridge's infantry, which acted as the rearguard. During the two days of fighting, Kelley had two horses killed under him.

The hornets' nest at Shiloh. Kelley escorted to the rear the U.S. soldiers captured here.

On April 8, Forrest ambushed the rather halfhearted Union pursuit at a place called "fallen timbers," the location of a prewar logging operation. About noon, a battalion of the 4th Illinois Cavalry, advancing down the Ridge Road, came up with the Confederate rearguard under Forrest. Two companies of the 77th Illinois Infantry were deployed to support the cavalry as the force started across a muddy stream crossing. Seeing some confusion in the Union cavalry, Forrest ordered a charge by the men under his command, mostly Texas Rangers with one company of Mississippi cavalry and one company from John Hunt Morgan's command. It appears that Kelley, temporarily in command, was ordered to hold Forrest's regiment in reserve. As the Confederates charged over the crest leading down to the stream crossing, the Union infantry fired a volley and came to "charge bayonets." Forrest's men came on to within twenty-five yards and then opened fire at their stationary enemies with shotguns and pistols, a large volume of fire for the number of men involved. The Union force broke for the rear, and the Confederates pursued. Forrest got too far in advance of his own men and was shot at point-blank range by a Union soldier, the ball passing through his hip and lodging against his spinal column. Forrest escaped in an almost miraculous fashion, another example of the inaccuracy of rifle fire in a confused situation, but the wound was painful and dangerous. The result of this wound was that Forrest had to turn command of the regiment over to Kelley.[40]

Fallen timbers. Kelley held the 3rd Tennessee in reserve while Forrest charged the U.S. pursuit. This angle is looking from the CS toward the U.S. position.

Kelley led the regiment to the vicinity of Mickies Crossroads to do picket duty and to keep an eye on a Confederate hospital that also contained wounded Union prisoners. This duty led to a series of reports to higher officers that reveal much about the state of both armies following Shiloh and also tell a good deal about the routine duties of a cavalry officer on picket duty:

April 10, 1862
General,
Being relieved on yesterday from the command at Gains Hill near Mickey's, I beg the honor to make the following mention of facts to the general commanding.
The communication for Major Genl Grant received the day before was conveyed to our lines, when the officer conveying it found two messengers from Genl Grant under a flag of truce awaiting a reply to a communication from the Federal lines of several days previous. The officer passed to the enemy's pickets about six hundred yards from our pickets when he met Maj. Murray of Col. Jackson's cavalry who proposed very courteously that Genl

Grant's messengers should convey the communication adding that it would be the most speedy arrangement. As he insisted the officer remained at the picket waiting from 3 P.M. till dark when he returned to my quarters. I sent him to the enemy's lines the next morning but he had not returned when I was relieved.

I had just before the arrival of the messages from the Genl commanding sent to the Federal lines the stipulations signed by Surgeon Rumbaugh (Federal) and Avert (Confederate) in relation to wounded prisoners of both armies at Genl Hardee Hospital approved by Genl Breckenridge. Genl Buell's reply in the hands of Colonel Wheeler wished to make the same stipulations in reference to this Hospital which had been agreed to for the General Hospital in front of Gains Hill—Hardee's Hospital being to the rear. This proposition I transmitted to my superior officer that your attention might be called to it. For several days the enemy's ambulances and wagons were allowed to pass our pickets to the front of the General Hospital bringing provisions and carrying off the wounded. The Arkansas Hospital a little to the front and right of the above Hospital sent in on Sunday a flag saying they were suffering for provisions—the bearer added

Mickie's Crossroads, the site of Kelley's outpost duty at the Confederate hospitals.

that a wagon would be allowed to pass with a flag of truce to the Hospital. I started supplies, they were assisted by a picket standing in sight and to the rear of the Hospital. The enclosed note was sent with the above mentioned agreement of the surgeons explains itself.

Our pickets have stood for several days within eight hundred yards of each other. They have ordered their pickets not to fire on ours unless we commence killing pickets which I ordered our pickets not to do.

Your Obedient Servant
D.C. Kelley, Lt. Col, Comding
Forrest's Cavalry Regiment
P.S. The note above mentioned was sent by the hands of Col. Wheeler, I simply reported to allow supplies to pass to causalities in Hospitals between our lines.

The matter was revisited a little later in the report Kelley filed with General Breckenridge:

Corinth April 19th 1862
Sir   Major Genl Breckenridge Commanding
The undersigned beg leave to submit the following report of the service rendered by Forrest Regiment of Cavalry at the out post near the "Mickey House."

Colonel Forrest having been wounded in a skirmish on Sunday evening with an advanced party of the enemy, I conducted the Regiment to the field under your orders to report to Colonel Wirt Adams. After remaining on this line for several hours, the enemy having fallen back, we retired to Monterey for forage for our horses having been without since Sunday night. On the next evening reported again for duty and stood the whole regiment on Wednesday night three miles in advance of the post, remained in the field in line until relieved the next day when Company H and I was detailed to carry off the wounded from the surrounding hospitals. The command remained at that post until the Tuesday following with most of the men constantly on duty. Our pickets for the whole line was Forrest's Regiment, standing within eight hundred yards of the enemy's pickets but prepared to fall back should our weakness be discovered, discretion being the best policy when knowledge of our exposed condition would have resulted in being liable to being cut off at any place. Captain Morgan's cavalry reporting, one hundred sixty five men present for duty and our regiment six hundred and fifty, supported by about eighty infantry succeeded in occupying the position. Hearing that your whole command was at Mickey's and Genl Bragg with a large force at Monterey.

The one incident concerning the management of our force I would call to your attention—for several days hence the arrangement agreed to by yourself of the ambulance and wagons of the enemy have been allowed with a white flag to pass our pickets to and from the General Hospital. On Sunday a messenger from the Arkansas Hospital reported that the wounded there suffered for supplies. The Federal pickets had sent papers to that Hospital. I sent supplies under a white flag. This was stopped just as it reached the hospital and Genl Buell refused us permission to send more, returning those sent.

You are no doubt aware of the kind of arrangements which you approved for Genl Hardee's Hospital. When refused by Genl Buell I was prevented from performing the same arrangement for the Hospitals which had been all the time in the rear of the lines and that had been made for the General Hospital which has been alternately captured by each party.

Your Obedient Servant
D.C. Kelley   Lt. Col. Comding Forrest Regiment Cavalry CSA
J.P. Strange, Adjutant[41]

KELLEY IN COMMAND

Forrest would be absent for three weeks while his wound was being treated, and Kelley's conduct of the regiment was a mixture of the daring action he had learned from Forrest and routine picketing duty imposed by the military situation of both armies. J.F. Fore, a private in the unit, recalled that Kelley led part of the men on a scout to determine the intentions of the Union army. Attacking the main concentration of Union infantry Kelley found the U.S. force immovable and too numerous to move. With enemy units swarming around him, Kelley broke up the reconnaissance force into small groups and told each one to make its way back toward Corinth on its own. Kelley himself led out three men and found all who had not become causalities of the fight had escaped. Kelley responded to their escape by holding religious services, at which he delivered the sermon.[42]

Forrest returned to the regiment around May 1, but his wound had not healed and the ball was still lodged near his spine. The pain Forrest experienced in riding horseback was too severe to be borne, so the decision was made for Dr. J.B. Cowan, the physician for the regiment, to remove the ball. Cowan was a skilled surgeon, having graduated from both the Medical College of Philadelphia and the Medical College of New York. He was the son of the Reverend Montgomery Cowan, who had been the legal guardian of Mary Montgomery prior to her marriage to Bedford Forrest. The operation was performed at Corinth, and Forrest took another two weeks of medical absence, leaving Kelley in command of the regiment. By the time Forrest returned, Beauregard had determined to have him promoted and sent to middle Tennessee and north Alabama to organize cavalry units there into a brigade and to place them on a combat-ready footing.[43]

The weeks following Shiloh were a strange time for Forrest's regiment with Kelley in command. The Union army moved forward slowly under the command of Henry Halleck, who replaced Ulysses Grant. Halleck sent large parties of infantry to advance a few miles each day, entrenching at the end of each advance. This left little room for action by the cavalry of either side. As a result, Kelley led the regiment in some scouting, but much of the time was spent in drill and training. The ponderous Union advance finally came close enough to Corinth that the Confederates evacuated the town on May 29, 1862, with the cavalry providing a rearguard. Ten days later, the Southern force established a new base at Tupelo, Mississippi, some fifty miles south and east of Corinth. On June 15, General Beauregard took sick leave, and the command passed to Braxton Bragg.

Confederate headquarters in Corinth, where Kelley sent reports of his cavalry scouts.

Kelley's men were sent to the northeast corner of Mississippi and the adjacent part of Alabama to guard the line of the Tennessee River and to harass Union troops who were becoming active in that area. In the subsequent reorganization of forces following the evacuation of Corinth, the cavalry in that sector came under the command of Frank Crawford Armstrong, a man who had the distinction of serving on both sides during the war. At First Manassas, Armstrong had been an officer in the United States army; resigning soon after that battle, he came south and offered his services to the Confederacy, where he was made welcome.

Following Shiloh, the Union troops had once more expanded their area of occupation into middle Tennessee and north Alabama. As part of Armstrong's force, Kelley and his men had the duty of picketing the southern banks of the Tennessee River in an attempt to prevent Federal crossings that could put additional pressure on the Confederate position at Tupelo. The cavalrymen were also attempting to protect the fertile farmlands of the Tennessee Valley so that the food supplies from that region could serve Confederate needs.

In late July, around the twenty-second of the month, Braxton Bragg conceived and implemented one of his best strategic ideas of the war. Bragg decided to utilize the railroads to shift his men from the northern area of Mississippi to Chattanooga, Tennessee. With rail transportation, he could make this move before his Union opponents could react to counter him. From Chattanooga, Bragg, in company with Kirby Smith, could strike north and northwest across middle Tennessee into Kentucky. This would be a giant flanking move that would take Bragg into the Federal rear and force a Union evacuation of much of the territory seized since February 1862. This move was made feasible by the successful attack Bedford Forrest had made on Murfreesboro, Tennessee, on July 13, an attack that caused the Union leader, Don Carlos Buell, to stop his movement toward Chattanooga and pull back to protect his supply lines.

While Bragg sent his infantry via Mobile and Montgomery, Alabama, to Atlanta, Georgia, and, finally, to Chattanooga, Tennessee, the cavalry, artillery and wagon trains of the army were to move across north Alabama, generally following the line of the Tennessee River, to reach Chattanooga. For this move to be feasible, the Union troops would have to be forced from the area between Tuscumbia and Decatur, Alabama. The key to forcing such a withdrawal would be to destroy bridges on the Memphis & Charleston Railroad so as to make direct communications impossible between the U.S. forces headquartered at Huntsville, Alabama, and those at Corinth, Mississippi. Since the supply and communication routes of the troops at Huntsville were already under pressure to the north and east, thanks to the success of Forrest's Murfreesboro attack a move to destroy connections with Corinth would make the position at Huntsville even less tenable and would exert pressure to withdraw from all of north Alabama.

Kelley, as part of Armstrong's force, was sent from Tupelo to Moulton, Alabama, reaching there on July 24, 1862. The target for this force was a trestle on the M&C near Courtland, Alabama, as well as several small bridges between Courtland and Decatur. There were two companies of the 10th Kentucky Infantry, U.S., and one company of the 1st Ohio Cavalry guarding the trestle. Moving forward on July 25, Armstrong sent Kelley and 140 men to flank the position to the west while another force was sent to the east. Taking the balance of his men, about 550 in all, Armstrong dismounted some men armed with rifles to bring the Yankees under fire while his flanking parties closed in. When the dismounted men opened fire, the Kentucky infantry took cover on the north side of the railroad, using the embankment as a breastwork. Kelley charged the 1st Ohio and "nearly annihilated it." The flanking parties then crossed the railroad and closed in from each end of the Union line. With the embankment no longer providing cover, the Kentucky infantry broke into the woods and were all captured.

The Confederates then burned the trestle and moved east toward Decatur. As they advanced, they skirmished with detachments from the 10th Indiana and the 31st Ohio Infantry Regiments. These units offered little resistance, except for a sharp skirmish with the Ohio men that left half that small force dead and wounded. At the end of the day, the entire Tennessee River had been cleared of Union forces between Tuscumbia and Decatur, Alabama. The Tuscumbia force was isolated, and the Huntsville garrison now had little reason to hold its position, so by the end of the week north Alabama was mostly devoid of U.S. forces. The work Kelley had helped accomplish at Courtland had opened the way for the move to Chattanooga.[44]

So far, David Kelley was having a good war. Since leaving Huntsville with the Kelley Troopers, he had advanced in rank from captain to lieutenant colonel; from the inexperienced leader of raw recruits to the confident leader of veteran cavalrymen; from a peaceful Methodist minister to a man of war. But changes were coming. Already the unit known as Forrest's Regiment was being broken up. With Forrest on independent command, four companies of the unit had already been detached for special duty. Within a few days of the fighting at Courtland, the remainder would be broken into two battalions, one of Alabama troops and the other of Tennesseans. The unit would not again be regimental strength until 1864. For Kelley, an even bigger change was coming. His health collapsed. Kelley had typhoid fever.

Chapter 3

A Mysterious Interlude, then a Return to War

MEDICAL LEAVE

With the Tennessee River Valley secured between Tuscumbia and Decatur, Alabama, and with Union troops pulling out of the area in order to protect their supply line in Tennessee, a route that depended on control of the Nashville and Chattanooga Railroad, the Confederate cavalry could begin to operate against the U.S. forces in and around Corinth, Mississippi. The plan included a reorganization of forces followed by a move into west Tennessee to disrupt Yankee lines of supply in that area. As this plan began to be implemented, David Kelley submitted his resignation from the army. On August 18, 1862, Kelley sent a formal letter to General Samuel S. Cooper, adjutant general of all Confederate forces. This letter went up the chain of command, going first to Kelley's immediate superior officer, Frank Armstrong. Kelley wrote:

> *Having declined reelection in the organization of the Battalion organized today under Special Orders No. 17 from Brigade Hd Qrts I beg leave to resign the office of Lt. Col. of Cavalry which I now hold and beg as a noncombatant to be discharged from C.S.A. In declining further service in the army for the present I fulfill a pledge made twelve months since when I did not dream that my services would be needed for a longer period than twelve months, a pledge which was personally made and depriving me of service at a time when I should be glad to do my duty in our cause which I feel honor bound to keep.*[1]

When Kelley had enlisted in 1861, the usual term of enlistment was twelve months. The fact that his original term had expired is one of the factors alluded to in his letter of resignation, but there seems to have been more on his mind. Just what was the pledge that he had personally given and that he felt honor bound to keep? Perhaps Kelley had promised his wife that he would not leave her with their small children for longer than one year; perhaps he had promised the deacons of his congregation and his presiding bishop that he would not be away from his church for longer than that time. The fact is, we do not know what pledge Kelley had on his mind and conscience. What we do know is that his resignation was refused.

On August 20, Kelley sent to his superior officers a second communication, one that gave a more compelling reason for leaving the active service. On this occasion he wrote:

> *Brig. Genl Armstrong,*
> *Having been incapacitated during the past several weeks by severe attacks of camp fever I believe it to be absolutely necessary that I should absent myself from the army for a period of time sufficient for me to recover my health. Therefore I respectfully request a leave of absence.*

Accompanying this request was a statement signed by Dr. J.B. Cowan, the regimental surgeon. Cowan stated:

> *Lt Col D.C. Kelley having applied for a certificate with which to support his application for leave of absence I hereby certify that I have carefully examined this officer and find that he is unable to perform the duties of his office because of a severe case of typhoid fever which appears to be in an advanced condition. I therefore declare my belief that he will not be able to resume his responsibilities as Lt Col until he has recuperated for several months. I therefore recommend a leave of absence for the reasons stated previously.*

General Sterling Price, commanding the District of the Tennessee, endorsed the application on August 22, 1862, noting: "Approved and respectfully forwarded. Lt. Col. Kelley has been granted leave of absence until the pleasure of the doctor is known."[2]

Kelley went to Aberdeen, Mississippi, to receive medical care and stayed there for a month. He was anxious to return to his family home in Wilson County, Tennessee, since his wife and family were there, staying with his parents. Mannie and the children had been in Leeville since February. Kelley also knew a baby was due to be born in September. Kelley sent letters that were delivered in roundabout ways through U.S. lines, some of them taking weeks to arrive. He also sent verbal messages by wounded and sick Confederates going back to their homes to recuperate. The developing Kentucky Campaign was clearing most of Tennessee of U.S. troops, and Kelley's health finally allowed him to make the trip. He arrived at his parents' home on September 25. His mother recorded in her diary, "With gratitude we record the coming of our own beloved David this afternoon. God has brought him back in safety." About midnight on September 27, Mannie gave birth to a daughter, Elizabeth. David continued to suffer the results of his illness for several more days, but he was no doubt well satisfied to be at home.[3]

Arriving with Kelley was his personal aide, the Chinese boy called Charles Marshall, who seems to have been with Kelley throughout the entire time since the two had left Huntsville in 1861. At some point, Marshall was sent to stay with the family of the Reverend Mr. James William Lambuth of Denmark, Mississippi. Reverend Lambuth was also a missionary to China and was planning to return to that country, plans that were successfully carried out in 1864 by passing through the lines of the contending armies and going to New York, from which place fellow Methodists helped the Lambuth family and Charles Marshall find their way aboard a ship bound for China.[4]

Seeking a Safe Refuge

David Kelley remained in Wilson County, preaching on occasion, until October 28, 1862, when he returned to his "station," resuming pastoral duties in Huntsville, Alabama. His father went with him, but Mannie and the children remained in Tennessee for the time being. By November 12, the U.S. forces had returned to the Lebanon area, while the gray army took up positions around Murfreesboro. This meant Kelley's home was behind Union lines. The Federal commander in nearby Gallatin was a fanatical individual named Eleazar Paine, who had the nasty habit of summarily killing Confederates who came into his hands. On December 10, Mannie and the children, assisted by the Reverend John Kelley, left on the dangerous and difficult journey to Huntsville, Alabama. They seem to have gone east from Lebanon before turning south through a no-man's land patrolled by both sides but occupied by neither. Reaching McMinnville, Tennessee, the family would be within Confederate lines and would have rail connections with Huntsville.

All attention in north Alabama was focused on Forrest at the end of April and the first days of May 1863 as "the wizard of the saddle" pursued and captured Union raiders under Able Streight. Following that victory, Forrest was the hero of the day. Forrest passed through Huntsville as he led his men back to middle Tennessee, and the *Huntsville Confederate* reported on May 18:

> *On Saturday last, in the presence of a large assembly of our citizens an elegant bay horse, of the best Virginia stock, was presented to Brig. Gen. Forrest in the name of the citizens of Huntsville and Madison county in humble testimony of their appreciation of his high military skill and prowess and of their gratitude to him and his gallant followers for deliverance from Yankee invasion and dominion. Mayor Coltart introduced him, and Col. J.J. Donegan made the presentation speech. Rev. Dr. Kelley (once Lt. Col.) made an eloquent eulogy on Gen. Forrest.*[5]

Happy days in Huntsville did not last much longer. By July 4, the Confederate forces under General Braxton Bragg had evacuated their base at Tullahoma, Tennessee, and were in retreat for Chattanooga. With middle Tennessee again in Northern hands, it was only a question of a few days before north Alabama was reoccupied. Once more the Kelley family would become refugees. The family moved first to Guntersville, Alabama, where David preached in the Methodist church. The family was there for some time because another Methodist minister, a Dr. Barr, reported to Margaret Kelley that her son was leading a revival there.

While the Kelleys were in Guntersville, the Army of Tennessee maneuvered and skirmished with its Union opponent, the Army of the Cumberland, for several weeks before the two forces clashed in a decisive fashion on September 18–20 at Chickamauga Creek. This was the first clear-cut Confederate victory in a major battle in the West, and it was followed by a semi-siege of the survivors of the Army of the Cumberland at Chattanooga. In November, Union forces under Ulysses Grant broke their way into the city and, at the Battle of Missionary Ridge, forced the Confederate forces into retreat into north Georgia. Sometime during this series of events, Kelley returned to the army camps, although he did not resume active duty. In a letter written to John Johnson in 1902, Kelley noted, "Forrest left me behind when he left Bragg's army...I joined Forrest at Jackson [Tennessee] on his second campaign in West Tennessee."[6] Forrest confronted Bragg in a famous interview in October 1863. During their conversation, largely one-sided, Forrest was frankly insubordinate and threatened Bragg's life. There had already been requests from civilians in Mississippi for Forrest to be sent into that area, and this was done in late October, with Forrest arriving in that state on November 18, 1863. By saying that "Forrest left me behind when he left Bragg's army," Kelley indicates that he was present near Chattanooga in October–November. However, there is no mention of Kelley in the *Official Records* as serving in any official capacity. Forrest took with him to Mississippi McDonald's Battalion, the nucleus of what was called "Forrest's Old Regiment," the unit Kelley had commanded as lieutenant colonel in 1862. Kelley was not on the roll of the battalion at the time it left with Forrest.

In 1892, Mrs. Irby Morgan published a book of wartime memories. She was the wife of a prominent Nashville businessman who had strongly supported the move for Southern independence. When Nashville came under Union occupation in 1862, the Morgan family had gone south as refugees. In the winter of 1863–64, Mrs. Morgan stated that David Kelley was in the army camps around Dalton serving as one of the many ministers who were preaching to the troops there. Kelley reviewed this book in the pages of the *Confederate Veteran* when the book was first published. He highly recommended the book; therefore, he was familiar with the author placing him in Dalton and he said nothing to contradict that assertion.[7]

Kelley, in his 1902 letter to John Johnson, stated, "I joined Forrest at Jackson." Forrest left Mississippi for west Tennessee in late March 1864 and made his headquarters at Jackson, Tennessee. On April 12, Forrest attacked and captured the U.S. garrison at Fort Pillow. Immediately on returning from that expedition, Forrest telegraphed Lieutenant General Polk at Demopolis, Alabama, that "Lieutenant-Colonel Kelley, of my old regiment, arrived yesterday from Tuscumbia." One of the Confederate casualties from Fort Pillow was an officer named Wiley Reed, prewar pastor of the Cumberland Presbyterian Church in Nashville. Reed died of his wounds in Jackson on May 2, 1864, and his good friend David Kelley conducted his funeral there.[8] This was an ironic duty, as Kelley would later learn. On the day Kelley conducted the funeral of his friend in Jackson, his own father, John Kelley, died at his home in Leeville, many miles to the east. The record of the funeral at Jackson places Kelley back with Forrest, but Kelley is not listed in any records as being in command of troops while at Jackson, so his position must have been that of volunteer aide.

RETURN TO ACTIVE DUTY

On May 14, 1864, General James R. Chalmers, commanding a division in Forrest's force, sent forward through the chain of command a letter to General Samuel Cooper, the adjutant general of all Confederate forces. Chalmers said: "I have the honor to ask that you will forward the commission for the field officers of the Tenn Batt which is the remnant of the regiment raised and commanded by Maj. Genl. Forrest and to ask that the battalion will be properly numbered and designated. The muster rolls are herewith furnished. Lt. Col. D.C. Kelley—Born in Tenn and resident of Alabama." Forrest promptly endorsed the document the same day and sent it on to General S.D. Lee, commander of the department. Lee returned the request with the note that the date of Kelley's election as lieutenant colonel had to be determined. On May 15, Kelley responded:

> *The Battalion designated McDonald's Battalion is part of "Forrest's Regiment Cavalry" as originally organized and commanded by Col. N.B. (Maj. Genl.) Forrest of which I was Lt. Col. from the organization. I continued with the Regiment after the promotion of Genl Forrest until relieved from duty on account of ill health. Four of the companies are now with the 4th Ala Regiment Cavalry. Co. A, a Kentucky company, has been detached. Co. I, when last heard from, was detached for conscript duty. If the Regiment has ever been dissolved by order of the Sect of War it is unknown alike to the undersigned and to Maj Genl Commanding I, on the recovery of my health, have been reordered by Maj Genl Forrest to the command of the Regiment and herewith ask for information from the Sect of War as to the detached companies.*

The matter of making formal Kelley's position moved slowly through the channels of the bureaucracy of the Confederate War Department, although Kelley exercised command during the interval. On September 7, 1864, Kelley again addressed a letter to the adjutant's office:

> *I have the honor to reply to your inquiry as to the date of my election to the Lt Colonecy of Forrest's Regiment. That the regiment had only two field officers of which I was second in command until April 3rd, 1862, when under orders of Genl A.S. Johnston an election was held at Burnsville, Mississippi, resulting in my promotion from Maj, to Lt. Col. At the reorganization of the regiment the field officers were retained in their former status. Save when absent on leave from disability I have commanded the regiment since the promotion of Genl N.B. Forrest.*

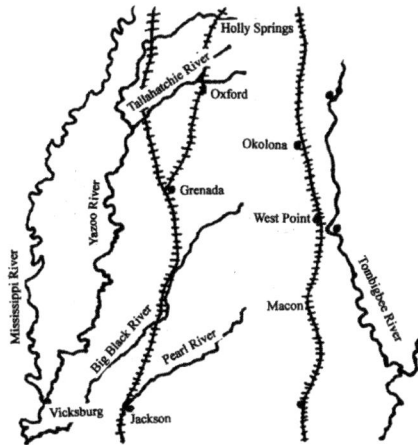

MISSISSIPPI 1864

Mississippi area of operations for Kelley, 1864. *Map by Martha Bradley.*

That seemed to satisfy the desk-bound warriors in Richmond and elsewhere for an official letter of appointment, as lieutenant colonel of the unit was issued to Kelley on November 23, 1864. His rank was to date from April 3, 1862.[9] The twelve months from May 1864 until May 1865 would mark a return to war, a war increasingly desperate for Kelley and the men with whom he served.

Kelley accompanied Forrest as the command returned to Mississippi in early May. Most of the rest of that month was spent in the vicinity of Tupelo, as Forrest saw to the reorganization, equipping and training of his men. One purpose of the move into west Tennessee had been to collect supplies and recruits, and in this Forrest had been successful. Many of the men he collected were fighters, being members of partisan units, but they were not trained cavalry soldiers, so Forrest had need of men like Kelley to assist in hammering these fighters into soldiers. Forrest also paid attention to the arming of these men, collecting three thousand weapons from Confederate authorities in Alabama as well as distributing those he had captured during his stay in west Tennessee. It was also necessary to reorganize the command. As noted, many of the men gathered were members of partisan units and had experience in fighting, but their units were too small for tactical purposes. These bands had to be amassed into battalions, regiments and brigades, with the whole then assigned to divisions. This reorganization would take time and would see small units shifted two or three times, in some cases, before a permanent home was found for them. As the shape of the new cavalry command took form, the men were somewhat dispersed to communities near Tupelo so as to make feeding men and horses easier.

BRICE'S CROSS ROADS

On May 23, news reached Forrest that a Union force was moving across north Alabama via the Tennessee River Valley, probably on its way to Rome, Georgia, to reinforce Sherman's drive toward Atlanta. It was also possible that all, or part, of this force could be sent south toward the iron-producing area of Alabama near Elyton (today called Birmingham). To harass this move toward Rome, and to guard against any raid into central Alabama, Forrest dispatched a division under General James A. Chalmers to Montevallo, Alabama. Phillip Roddey was also sent to worry the Union force going toward Rome. This move divided Forrest's manpower in half, with only about five thousand left in Mississippi.

Although the 26th Tennessee Battalion was part of Chalmers's division sent to Montevallo, it seems that Kelley was not yet attached to that unit. As U.S. general S.D. Sturgis began the move that would culminate in the Battle of Brice's Cross Roads. Kelley was doing courier duty for Forrest. In a postwar letter to Dr. John Allan Wyeth, Kelley said that on June 8 he was sent with a dispatch from Forrest to Colonel W.A. Johnson, who commanded a brigade in Roddey's division. Johnson was ordered to move as quickly as possible to join Forrest near the town of Baldwin or near Brice's Cross Roads.[10] Johnson's men played a vital role in the battle of June 10, and it would be a great surprise if Kelley had not returned to the field of battle with the men he had been sent to fetch. However, there is no mention of Kelley in the official reports filed by Forrest about the Battle of Brice's Cross Roads, thus reinforcing the assumption that Kelley was still functioning as a volunteer aide. Whatever role Kelley may have played, he always seemed justly proud of the victory the outnumbered Confederates won that day. The battle was a sterling example of a numerically smaller force defeating twice its numbers by utilizing the road net, topography and weather, forcing the enemy to arrive on the field in disjointed units that could be defeated in detail. In 1900, Kelley took the lead in organizing a reunion of Forrest's men at Brice's Cross Roads.[11]

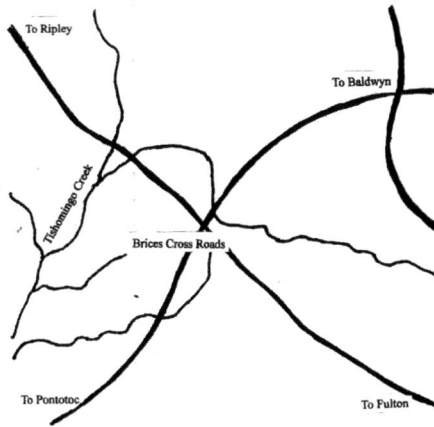

BRICES CROSS ROADS

Brice's Cross Roads, site of Forrest's greatest victory. *Map by Martha Bradley.*

After his stunning victory on June 10, Forrest again reorganized his command, continuing the process of consolidating small commands. On July 18 and 19, a flurry of orders re-created a fabled unit and placed Kelley in command of it. A company of scouts commanded by a Captain Morphis was ordered to report to Kelley. At the same time, seven companies that had been the 26th Battalion of Tennessee Cavalry were placed under Kelley's command, and the consolidated unit was again to be called the Third Tennessee (Forrest's) Regiment. The regiment was assigned to Neely's Brigade.[12] After an absence of more than two years, "Forrest's Old Regiment" was a regiment again, and David C. Kelley was once more in command.

TUPELO

The orders of July 18 and 19 made official an arrangement that had been in place for several days. As the campaign that led to the battle at Tupelo—sometimes called the Battle of Harrisburg—began, Kelley was in command of the 3rd Tennessee Cavalry, although the command was referred to in communications as "Forrest's Old Regiment." For at least part of the campaign, Kelley also had under his command the 1st Mississippi Partisan Rangers.

By the time Brice's Cross Roads had been fought, the armies commanded by William Sherman were deep in Georgia, fighting fiercely to work their way closer to Atlanta. Sherman depended utterly on the Nashville & Chattanooga Railroad to bring ordnance supplies to his force. Every day ten trains, each consisting of ten boxcars loaded with ammunition, left Nashville for the all-day journey to Chattanooga.[13] From Chattanooga, the ordnance supplies made their way down the Atlantic & Western as far as possible and then by wagon to the fighting front. Sherman's armies could live for a time off the countryside, but no Minié balls grow in Georgia. The rails had to remain intact for bullets to arrive for the bluecoats. No sooner were Sturgis and his survivors back in Memphis than Sherman in desperation ordered Andrew Jackson Smith to take another expedition into Mississippi and hunt down Forrest. A.J. Smith was well aware that hunting down Forrest was one thing; what to do when he found him was quite another. The order for this expedition was given on June 16, but it was not until June 27 that Smith united his infantry with his cavalry under Grierson at the town of Salsbury.[14]

Thanks to the activities of his scouts under Jessie Forrest, Bedford Forrest was well aware of the projected U.S. move. He accordingly assembled his troops around Okolona so as to have good roads by which to move against the attack and to be able to protect the food-producing "black prairie" region south of Tupelo. Chalmers brought his division back from Alabama and soon received orders to have a special strike force composed of the 3rd and 7th Tennessee Regiments ready to move at "an hours notice." This was to be the advance guard that would meet and delay Smith's move. That move came on July 6, and Kelley was ready to meet it on July 7, although he moved into battle with the 1st Mississippi Partisan Rangers replacing the 7th Tennessee. Also in the force was Forrest's Escort Company, the personal bodyguards of Nathan Bedford Forrest. This was the first time Kelley had gone into combat with this group of men who had become a legend in the western theater of the war, but the relationship between Kelley and the Escort would be long lasting. After the war, the survivors of the Escort Company formed a veterans' association, and Kelley was one of a select number of non-Escort members invited to join the association.[15]

The U.S. advance came down the Ripley Road and was led by six companies of the 2nd Iowa Cavalry commanded by Colonel D.E. Coon. In position along Whitten's Branch were the 3rd Tennessee and the 1st Mississippi Partisan Rangers. Although called "partisan rangers," the 1st Mississippi was actually a regular cavalry company whose original commanding officer had been Colonel William Falkner, the great-grandfather of the writer of the same name (the writer added a "u" to the spelling of his surname). Kelley confronted the Iowa troopers from a strong position and held up the U.S. advance for two hours, fighting a sharp skirmish. In the end, more Union troops arrived, and Kelley had to pull his men back. During the night, the blue forces reached Ripley.[16]

As the U.S. forces occupied Ripley, Kelley observed that the attitude of the Union soldiers had become much more harsh toward Southern civilians. When Kelley had taken medical leave in 1862, there had already been incidents of wanton destruction directed against civilians simply because they were pro-Confederate. Now Kelley watched as all the public buildings in Ripley, including churches, went up in smoke, deliberately burned as an act of punishment against the population who supported the fierce fighters who rode with Forrest. Among those fighters was the original commander of the 1st Mississippi, Colonel Falkner of Ripley. That fire spread to many homes, reducing the town to ashes before daybreak.[17]

General A.J. Smith had a good deal of respect for the fighting ability of Forrest and his men. He was also a good student of the mistakes made by his predecessor at Brice's Cross Roads, so Smith did not allow his command to become strung out along the roads. By advancing slowly, Smith kept his troops well in hand but also gave the Confederates an opportunity to prepare to meet him. Part of this preparation was the fortification of Okolona by the Confederates, a destination toward which Kelley fell back in hopes of drawing Smith into that area. Smith had no wish to accommodate Kelley, and when brought to a standstill by the constant skirmishing, the Union forces took a side road that led to Tupelo. This was a very good strategic move, stealing a march on Forrest and allowing Smith to select the position in which to fight.

As the move was made toward Tupelo, Kelley led the 3rd Tennessee and the Escort Company in pursuit. Along the banks of Miller's Creek, the 61st USCT (U.S. Colored Troops) and the 2nd U.S. Colored Artillery made a stand. After sharp skirmishing, the Union troops fell back, with the 61st USCT being relieved by the 59th. Again the two forces clashed, but Kelley did not have enough force to break the Union rearguard. Even when Rucker's Brigade of Forrest's command struck the right flank of the U.S. column, the march was not stopped.[18] Smith was determined to reach Tupelo.

Ever since the fighting that took place on July 14 and 15, controversy has swirled around the decision of the Confederates to attack. It was clear that, having been brought to a halt, Smith could not remain where he was for any length of time; he would have to force his way forward or fall back to Memphis. Either of these eventualities would have offered the Confederates a good opportunity to fight at an advantage to themselves. Both Lieutenant General S.D. Lee and Forrest understood the strength of the position Smith had occupied. They both also knew that other U.S. forces were threatening their theater of operations so that action against Smith needed to be swift and decisive. Many writers have argued that Forrest opposed the attack against such a strong position as a matter of general principles, while others have argued that Forrest cooperated with Lee in fighting the battle. Kelley shed no light on this matter, either at the time of the fight or in his later writings. The 3rd Tennessee was in one of the hottest spots in the battle and was pinned down under fire for a considerable time. Their action can be summed up as advancing, taking cover and enduring until they could fall back. After dark, Kelley's command was involved in an attempt to turn the left flank of the Northern line, but this only led to a great deal of blind firing in the dark.[19] On the fifteenth, Smith decided to withdraw from his lines, being short of both food and ammunition. As the Union force crossed Oldtown Creek, the brigade of Tyree Bell fell on its rearguard, only to find itself in difficulty. Chalmers led his brigade to the rescue, but the situation was so desperate he was forced to commit his men to the fight as each regiment came up. Kelley knew this was not good tactics, as did Chalmers, but there was no alternative. The predictable result was that Bell was rescued but the Yankees escaped.[20] There was no close pursuit as the blue column receded toward Memphis.

The Confederate action during the whole campaign had been disjointed and lacking in strength. The attrition of men and horses was having the inevitable effect of leaving the Southern army able to fight but too weak to win decisively. As a patriot, this was a difficult fact for Kelley to accept, but his logical mind forced him to deal with the obvious facts. Strategic planning was more important than ever before since the tactical ability of his men was becoming limited.

OXFORD AND THE MEMPHIS RAID

The exhaustion of the Confederates was not to be relieved by Yankee inactivity. No sooner had A.J. Smith arrived back in Memphis than he was ordered to begin organizing another expedition to fight Forrest. The first move for Smith came on July 29 as he prepared two infantry divisions and four thousand cavalry, a total of about fourteen thousand men, to move to Grand Junction and, as soon as the railroad could be repaired, to go forward to Holly Springs.

While the U.S. forces were busy in Memphis, Forrest was again reorganizing his command. Kelley and the 3rd Tennessee found itself themselves in Rucker's Brigade, which was temporarily commanded by Colonel James J. Neely. The reorganization of Forrest's cavalry did nothing to solve the major problem facing everyone from the commanding general to the enlisted men—there was too much territory for the available manpower to cover. The Confederate strength had to be stretched thinly to watch all the possible routes of advance from Memphis to the food-producing areas of Mississippi. Stephen Dill Lee, as department commander, had an even greater problem. His area of responsibility was threatened not only from U.S. forces at Memphis but also from troops at Vicksburg, Port Hudson and just offshore at Mobile. Lee could not afford to strip any area of many men to reinforce Forrest.

The U.S. forces took more than a week to move from Memphis through Grand Junction and on toward Holly Springs. As the blue troops advanced, Chalmers found himself facing a Union cavalry force under Colonel J.J. Woods. Although Chalmers said he needed more men to watch this prong of the advance, Forrest had none to spare him until the direction of the main Union blow could be determined. Chalmers did not have the men and resources to stop Woods, and the Union cavalry entered the university town of Oxford on August 9, 1864. This was to be a short stay, less than twenty-four hours, but it marked the beginning of several days of fighting around Oxford, during which the town would change hands several times and would suffer destruction from fires set by the U.S. forces, as well as looting of private homes and businesses.

While Chalmers was trying without success to stop the Union advance toward Oxford, Kelley's 3rd Tennessee was in company with the 7th Tennessee, holding a picket line along the Tippah River above Pontotoc. This task force was sent to the Tippah on August 4 and stayed there until August 11. This was necessary duty, but it was hot and boring, with the only excitement coming from frequent thunderstorms that doused the exposed bivouac. Running out of food and seeing no Yankees, the two regiments were ordered to fall back on Pontotoc on August 11.[21] The demands being made on Forrest's men are obvious from what happened next. At 2:00 a.m. on August 13, Kelley was ordered to take his 3rd Tennessee and move in conjunction with the 7th to wreck the railroad between Grand Junction and Holly Springs. With fourteen thousand Yankees moving against his smaller force, Forrest was using strategy in attempting to force the retreat he could not achieve tactically.

Kelley encountered problems almost immediately. He rapidly issued six days' food to his men but could find only two days' rations for the horses. He would have to spend time and effort supplying his horses from the country they were to enter. On reaching New Albany, Kelley found that Colonel William L. Duckworth refused to accompany the raid for reasons that were not specified. Since Duckworth was senior in rank to Kelley, it had been Kelley's expectation that Duckworth would take over command, but now he had to continue with less-than-adequate preparation. Kelley knew nothing about the target area and his men had no tools with which to damage the road once they reached it. Furthermore, Kelley had no artillery, and he had good reason to believe that all bridges and trestles were guarded by fortifications that were safe from attackers armed only with small arms. Finally, having been on picket duty for a week, Kelley did not have the latest reports on the location of the Union cavalry. Despite these problems, Kelley moved out as ordered. Progress was slow because of the necessity of sending out numerous small parties of scouts to secure accurate information as to the location and strength of Union forces. Many of the citizens were hesitant to talk with the Confederates, so harsh had been their treatment under the Union occupying force. The penalty for assisting the Confederates was the destruction of all buildings on a farm, including the house, and frequently, the householder was hanged in his own dooryard.

Not all the residents were intimidated. Whenever a Union force came into the area, it was typical for the Home Guard—as men too old or boys too young for regular military service were called—to rally with the assistance of any soldiers who might be at home on furlough or recuperating from sickness or wounds. L.R. Buress of Pontotoc was associated with one such group and noted that some twenty of his neighbors came together to harass the U.S. forces. They attacked groups of foragers, picked up stragglers and blocked roads as opportunity offered. This group captured and paroled over thirty Union soldiers, keeping their horses and weapons for themselves.[22]

Kelley led his men into Lamar, Mississippi, on the night of August 13–14, and they set to work to do such damage as they could. As most of the men worked at wrecking the track, Kelley and an advance party made a scout toward Holly Springs. Unknown to him, a party of some sixty men from the 7th Indiana Cavalry was approaching Kelley's flank under cover of darkness. Kelley was riding some yards behind his advance guard, and the Indiana troopers came into the road after the Confederates had passed and before Kelley arrived. Seeing some men ahead of him, Kelley ordered them to keep better ranks and to slow down. Immediately the Yanks obeyed this order, and as they did, the moon came from behind a cloud. By its light, Kelley saw that the nearest man was a Yankee sergeant. Without hesitating, Kelley drew his pistol and shot the man out of his saddle, calling on the 3rd Tennessee to charge. The second in command, Major P.T. Allin, was riding a mule, and his animal became unmanageable in the confusion. For a few seconds there was general confusion, but Kelley was soon rescued by a volley of pistol shots that, fortunately, missed him while disabling enough Yankees to send the rest into quick retreat.

Throughout the night, the work wrecking the road continued, and scouts came in with news of Union forces pressing in from all sides. A council of the officers of the two regiments agreed that there was no prospect of doing damage that could not be repaired quickly and that staying where they were invited capture. As day broke, Kelley led the men toward New Albany.[23] A brief rest was taken at that town while awaiting orders, but by August 18, Kelley had moved his men to Oxford, where he arrived "with men worn out and horses unfit for duty." Even so, the next day Kelley led his men to the front lines to confront the enemy who was moving in force on Oxford to occupy the town again. Kelley's report noted that this day was spent in a rainstorm so heavy that most of the time the men could only pop the caps on the nipples of their rifles without the cartridge firing and that the artillery "burst tubes"—that is, ignited the friction primers but without the powder firing. In such rain that weapons could not be fired, not much damage was done by either side. It was on this day that Oxford was occupied a second time and that Forrest led two thousand men around the Union right flank on a daring strike toward Memphis.[24]

Falling back to camp, Kelley was ordered to send out so many pickets that he had only seventy men left with the colors for duty the next day. With this scratch force, Kelley went back to the front lines the next day to help repel a reported Union advance that never materialized. This was just as well because, at one point, Kelley found that all the rest of the Confederate line had fallen back and he and his men were totally isolated. That night, Kelley led his men some five miles to the rear across the Yoncona River.

On August 21, A.J. Smith received news that Forrest had attacked Memphis the day before. Setting fire to the heart of the town, and turning a blind eye as his men looted homes and businesses, General Smith led the U.S. forces out of town. Kelley's command was among the pursuers.

Falling back along the road toward Memphis, the Union troops stopped at Abbeville, and Kelley caught up with them. At some point during the pursuit, Kelley had been given the 5th Mississippi Cavalry to add to the 3rd Tennessee's numbers. Advancing to an advantageous post, Kelley dismounted the 5th Mississippi and kept his men in the saddle. The response from the Union troops soon came in the form of three regiments of infantry. The fighting was hot and soon came to close quarters, with the blue infantry overlapping both flanks of the Confederate line. Kelley held on, hoping for reinforcements, but these did not arrive. At the last possible moment, he ordered the 5th Mississippi to fall back on their horse holders and used the Tennessee troopers to hold off the advancing Yanks. Kelley reported, "We held the position against three regiments of infantry until they had not only flanked us on both sides, but almost closed in our rear. When the order reached me to retire my flag (the staff and material of which are riddled with shot) was in forty paces of the flag of the advancing infantry." In this engagement the 5th Mississippi lost twenty-three men and the 3rd Tennessee five.[25]

Forrest's use of strategy had worked. The Union expedition withdrew from the agricultural heartland of Mississippi. But the strategy of the daring and picturesque raid on Memphis had been made possible only by the desperate fighting and physical sacrifices of commands like Kelley's who held the attention of the U.S. forces while Forrest outflanked them and rode into Memphis. The withdrawal of Smith marked the end of the summer of battles in Mississippi. The two infantry divisions commanded by Smith were sent to other areas, leaving Forrest free to do what he had been wanting to do—move into Tennessee to attack Sherman's rail link to Nashville. With Atlanta practically in Union hands, it might appear too late to accomplish any military objective, but such was not the case. At the beginning of the 1864 campaign, Sherman had been ordered to destroy the Confederate Army of Tennessee; the capture of Atlanta was a secondary objective. Even with the fall of Atlanta, Sherman would still be vulnerable, dangling at the end of a long and exposed supply line. If the Army of Tennessee were intact and could limit foraging by Sherman's forces, the destruction of the railroads could cause the Union forces to abandon Atlanta and make their way back to Chattanooga, a distance of more than one hundred miles. Making such a withdrawal through country already fought over and without adequate supplies could be very damaging to the Federal cause.

RAIDING THE RAILROADS

The first moves for the attack were made on September 16 when Kelley, leading Rucker's Brigade and the horses of Morton's and Walton's batteries, moved to Cherokee, Alabama. The guns and men of the artillery were to come by train via the Mobile & Ohio to Corinth and then the Memphis & Charleston, both of these roads having been repaired in preparation for the move. Working in conjunction with Roddey's command, Kelley helped make ready boats to cross the Tennessee at Colbert's Ferry while also collecting food and forage. Roddey sent men to secure the north bank of the river, and on September 20, dismounted men from all units crossed on the ferry. The next day, Forrest ordered his horsemen across the river, almost a mile wide at that point and crossable by a difficult ford whose winding path took advantage of the large slabs of flat rocks that made up the shoals in the river.

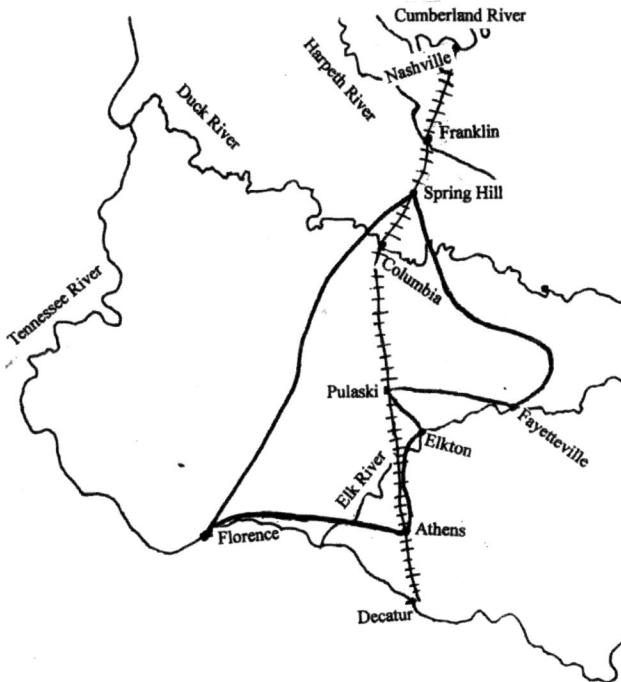

RAIDING THE RAILROAD

Raiding the railroads in an attempt to stop Sherman. *Map by Martha Bradley.*

Men, guns and wagons camped that night at Florence, having covered about twenty-five miles.[26]

The major objectives of this expedition were to attack Tennessee & Alabama Railroad, running from Nashville, Tennessee, to Decatur, Alabama, on the Tennessee River; and to then disrupt traffic on the Nashville & Chattanooga, which ran between those two cities. The T&A was a secondary line of supply for Sherman but was still significant. From Nashville, ammunition and food reached Decatur, where they were reloaded on steamboats for the trip up the Tennessee to Chattanooga. The use of this line reduced the traffic on the main line of supply, the N&C Railroad. Although the boats going to Chattanooga crossed under the bridge used by the N&C at Bridgeport, Alabama, the two routes operated independently of each other. Sherman was especially dependent on these rail lines for ordnance supplies.

Both these railroads were secured by Union garrisons placed in the larger towns and villages along their routes, and these were supplemented by earthworks and blockhouses guarding bridges, trestles and other important features. The blockhouses were built of heavy timbers that had been squared and arranged so as to resemble a giant log cabin. A ditch was dug around the outside of these works and the dirt piled against the logs, rendering them secure against rifle fire and even light artillery. Some of the larger blockhouses were two-story structures and were constructed in octagonal or cruciform shape as best suited the lay of the ground in their location. These structures were garrisoned by up to a company of infantry and might mount one or two small pieces of artillery. They were very effective protection for the railroad against bands of guerrillas and roving cavalry. The officers in command were under strict orders not to surrender when attacked but to hold their post until a relief column from the nearest garrison could reach them. General Grenville M. Dodge had overseen the construction of many of the blockhouses along the T&A and the N&C. In his autobiography, he stated that none of the blockhouses had ever been captured. This statement reflects a lapse of memory, since the blockhouses would offer little resistance as Forrest moved forward.

On the night of September 22, Kelley, in response to orders from Forrest, detached the 14th Tennessee Cavalry under Colonel White to join the 20th Tennessee, commanded by Jesse Forrest, to attack a horse corral between Athens and Decatur and to block the railroad there. Forrest needed the horses to mount some 400 of his men. The next morning, Kelley led the remainder of his men to Athens, where the town and its Union garrison were surrounded. The garrison took shelter in a large, well-constructed earthwork on the west side of town. The night of September 23 was spent getting the troops and artillery into position, and the attack on the garrison commenced on September 24. Forrest opened with his artillery at daylight and began to advance his men but decided to try his usual tactics of demanding a surrender before launching an attack. In a move that Forrest could have patented, he moved his artillery from place to place, mounted and then dismounted his men, marching them across open spaces where the Union commander could count them over and over, and convinced Colonel Wallace Campbell, 110th U.S. Colored Troops, to surrender. Wallace reported that he surrendered 538 men and 33 officers from the various commands making up the garrison.[27]

While the fighting and deception were going on around the fort, a train was heard coming from the direction of Decatur. Kelley was ordered to take the men under his command and to move in connection with Colonel Jesse Forrest to block the reinforcements that were thought to be on the train. The train, loaded with fresh Union troops, stopped about a mile southeast of the fort in the vicinity of a blockhouse guarding a small bridge over a creek and unloaded the men in a protected position, some of them in a shallow cut and others behind a long stack of cordwood that had been collected as fuel for the trains. Kelley led the 15th Tennessee and the 3rd to the attack, routing the defenders from their position along the railroad. As the Yankees fled toward the fort, they ran into Jesse Forrest's regiment, where they were surrounded and forced to surrender, but not before wounding Jesse Forrest. The nearby blockhouse then surrendered, and its small garrison joined the growing column of prisoners. Ironically, the Union reinforcements, the 102nd Ohio, were convinced to surrender by a Confederate prisoner. As the Ohio men ran toward the fort, they overran a part of the Confederate skirmish line, capturing Captain Henry C. Klyce. When Jesse Forrest surrounded the men pushing toward the fort, Klyce pointed out to the Union commander that the situation was hopeless and that he should surrender. The Union officer replied that he had no intention of putting his head up into the line of fire but that Klyce could if he wanted to. Klyce did so, surrendering the Yankee force on behalf of its commander.[28]

Kelley followed Forrest as the command moved immediately up the rail line toward Nashville. The next major objective was Sulphur Creek trestle, three hundred feet in length and seventy-two feet high. The command moved steadily, capturing blockhouses as they came to them, and confronted the fortifications at Sulphur Creek. There were two blockhouses situated in a ravine so as to protect the approaches to the ends of the trestle and an earthwork on a hill overlooking the entire site. For some reason, the Union earthwork was in a position overlooked by still higher hills in rifle range. Forrest immediately ordered his artillery to occupy these hills and, to protect the guns while they worked into position, sent Kelley to advance his men against the fort so they could sweep the parapet with rifle fire and prevent sharpshooters from shooting at the artillerymen and horses. As Kelley sent the 3rd Tennessee forward, they advanced against the 3rd Tennessee, U.S. Also in the garrison were troops of the 111th USCT and the 9th Indiana.

As Kelley's men advanced, one of them, Thomas D. Duncan, felt a premonition of death. This was something he had not experienced before, although he had enlisted in 1861 as a member of the original regiment commanded by Forrest, the regiment known as Forrest's Old Regiment or, officially, as the 3rd Tennessee Cavalry. Before the fight had gone on very long, Duncan was struck in the hand by a ball that penetrated between two of his knuckles, severely bruising his hand but without mangling it. Bleeding freely, Duncan made his way to the rear, where Kelley wrapped his hand in a handkerchief and sent him to the surgeon. Duncan, a veteran of three years of combat, had not yet reached his eighteenth birthday.[29]

Before the artillery opened, Forrest sent in his usual demand for surrender only to have it rejected by Colonel W.H. Lathrop of the USCT. Shortly after the bombardment opened, Lathrop was killed and Colonel J.B. Minnis of the 3rd Tennessee, U.S., was severely wounded. After about two hours of firing, Major Eli Lilly, 9th Indiana Cavalry, raised the white flag. Lilly would be involved in a curious incident in Mississippi while a prisoner of war. Coincidentally, many of those captured would be aboard the *Sultana* the next spring.[30]

Among those captured was an enlisted member of the 111th USCT named William Holland. Before the war, Holland had been a slave near Cowan, Tennessee. Dr. J.B. Cowan, chief surgeon of Forrest's command and a former resident of Cowan himself, recognized Holland following the surrender. Cowan appears to have had some personal tie with Holland because he requested that Holland not be sent to a POW camp but that he be made a hospital steward instead. Holland agreed. This kept Holland out of a prison camp and may well have saved his life.[31]

Forrest had now captured enough horses that all his men were mounted. On September 26, the command moved parallel to the railroad toward Pulaski. At Brown's plantation, a refugee camp was found with about two thousand Negroes occupying it. These were mostly old men, women and children, since the U.S. Army typically conscripted all able-bodied male

African Americans to do forced labor. Forrest evacuated the occupants of what he described as a "den of wretchedness" and burned the hovels composing the camp. Another blockhouse surrendered to the advance forces of which Kelley was a part, and the trestle over Richland Creek went up in flames, as had the bridges over Sulphur Creek and Elk River.[32]

Battle was joined near Pulaski on September 27. Kelley was now in command of Rucker's Brigade, and he advanced for several miles before fighting a sharp skirmish with part of the U.S. garrison of Pulaski. This skirmish checked the Confederate advance temporarily until General Buford led his brigade up. At Tarpley's Shop, the Kentucky troops under Buford lost ten men killed in ten minutes of fighting, an event that left an indelible impression on the minds of the survivors. No other event in the history of their units was the subject of so much discussion in the postwar pages of the *Confederate Veteran* as the death of these men. As the Confederates pushed on toward Pulaski, the fighting became general, with the Union soldiers attempting to throw forward their right flank to enfilade the Confederate troops in the center of the advancing Southern line. Kelley frustrated this attempt by leading his men in a rapid advance closely supported by the artillery accompanying him, this close artillery support being a tactic surely learned from observing Forrest do the same thing on so many fields. Kelley's attack sent the Union lines into a hasty retreat, which did not pause until the Yankees were safe behind the earthworks they had constructed around Pulaski. During this advance, a shell burst directly in the face of General Tyree Bell, temporarily taking him out of action but not hurting him seriously. An examination of the Federal fortifications convinced Forrest that an attack would not succeed. Waiting until after dark, the Confederates left campfires burning and faded away eastward toward Fayetteville with the intention of reaching the tracks of the Nashville & Chattanooga near Tullahoma.[33]

A torrential rain made the roads bottomless pools of mud and slowed the column. On September 28, Kelley reached Fayetteville and about noon on the next day stopped at Mulberry. There, Forrest received word that Union troops were moving from both Nashville and Chattanooga to reinforce Tullahoma and to strengthen the guards at all the bridges in the vicinity. With no likelihood of accomplishing anything against the Nashville & Chattanooga Railroad, Forrest sent Kelley and Buford toward Huntsville, Alabama, with about 1,500 men. They were to capture the town, if possible, damage the Memphis & Charleston Railroad and then cross the Tennessee River to its south bank and rejoin the main force somewhere in the vicinity of Florence, Alabama, about the location from which the raid had begun.

On reaching Huntsville, Kelley and Buford sent the commander of the U.S. garrison a Forrest-like demand for surrender but got the expected refusal. Firing a few rounds from their artillery to keep the Yankees on edge, the two withdrew along the rail line toward Madison, doing what damage they could before breaking away west for the crossing of the river. By October 6, Kelley was once more united with the rest of the command, at least for a short time. He did have the satisfaction of seeing in Forrest's report the words "I take pleasure also in calling the notice of the Government to the conduct of Colonel Kelley, commanding Colonel Rucker's brigade. He displayed all the dash, energy, and gallantry which has so long made him an efficient officer, and justly merits promotion by his Government."[34]

ENGAGEMENT AT EASTPORT

On October 9, Kelley received orders to take the brigade, which he commanded temporarily, and to move with one section of guns from Hudson's battery under Lieutenant Walton to Eastport, Mississippi. Forrest was resting his command at Cherokee, Alabama, but he had received word that a Union force was planning to land from boats at Eastport, move inland and cut the Memphis & Charleston Railroad, stranding all the locomotives and rolling stock Forrest was using around Cherokee to supply his command. The intelligence Forrest received was very good since the U.S. force ordered to undertake this mission had assembled at Clifton, Tennessee, on October 8. At Clifton, Colonel George B. Hoge was placed in command of his own regiment, the 113th Illinois, the 120th Illinois, the 61st USCT, some thirty dismounted Missouri cavalrymen and Company G, 2nd Missouri Light Artillery. Colonel Hoge was ordered to move to Eastport, seize the railroad and hold his position for two days until reinforced. He placed his command aboard the transports *Aurora*, *Kenton* and *City of Peking*. The gunboats *Key West* and *Undine* would provide protection for the move.[35]

Kelley arrived at Eastport on October 9 and scouted the probable field of battle, an area near the landing. The Tennessee River cuts deeply into the soil of Alabama and Mississippi before turning back north to flow through Tennessee to the Ohio River. This deep cutting means the surface of the river, in the days before TVA, was often twenty to thirty feet below the top of the riverbanks. Boats could land people and material only where a ravine cut through the riverbanks to provide a slope that could be climbed to the surrounding country. This meant Kelley knew where the U.S. troops would come ashore at Eastport. Overlooking the landing was an earthwork dating from much earlier in the war and abandoned for some time. Although eroded, the remnants of its parapet provided a masked location for one of the ten-pounder guns Lieutenant Walton had brought. The second gun was placed in a depression on the other side of the landing so that it was out of sight until run up into firing position. The two guns could put a crossfire on the landing. Kelley placed his dismounted men a few yards back from the place where the road from the landing reached the level top of the riverbanks, concealing them in the high weeds of an old field.

Colonel Hoge arrived at Eastport mid-morning on October 10. The *Key West* steamed past the landing and, seeing nothing, gave the signal to land. Two lieutenants were first over the landing stages and rode their horses to the top of the bank. This was the only scouting party Hoge sent out. A Confederate eyewitness recounted, "The three transports were blue with Yankees." As soon as the lieutenants had left the transports, the infantry began to surge ashore. The same Confederate eyewitness

Steamboat landing at Eastport, Mississippi, where Kelley defeated the U.S. landing party.

said, "As soon as the transports were made fast to the bank the stage planks were dropped and the soldiers began to disembark. Company after company marched ashore and we counted sixty horses and three cannon on the bank." Hoge sent the 61st USCT ashore, letting them do the dangerous work while keeping his two white regiments aboard the boats until the landing was secured. Just past the top of the riverbank the two scouts were fired on by Kelley's pickets, and as the scouts pelted back down the bank, Kelley's men surged to the top of the slope and opened fire. Walton's two guns did the same, with one of the first shots hitting and disabling the *Undine*. Hoge ordered the men ashore to form a battle line, although he was himself aboard the *Key West*. With the *Undine* out of action, the commanding officer of the *Key West* decided to depart the scene, leaving the infantry on shore and the transports without any covering fire. In quick order, Walton put a shell into a caisson aboard the *Kenton* and another shell into a caisson on the *Aurora*. With fires blazing on both these transports, Hoge gave the order for the *City of Peking* to withdraw, stranding his men and guns on shore. Kelley continued to pour in rifle fire as the Yankee cannon were abandoned and the infantry made a run down the narrow beach between the river and the bluffs bordering it. Hoge managed to reembark most of his muddy, wet men farther down the stream, but his artillery and wounded were left to Kelley. With a great deal of satisfaction with the neat trap he had sprung, Kelley reported seventy-four Union soldiers killed, wounded and captured, along with three guns and sixty horses with harness of the Missouri battery. Confederate losses were one man wounded.[36]

Kelley had been dealing with Yankee gunboats since 1861 and had long since lost his sense of awe at the appearance and firepower of these vessels. Kelley would deal with the U.S. Navy again on the Johnsonville expedition and at the Battle of Nashville. He and his men knew that the steep banks of the river made it impossible for the guns aboard the boats to hit targets near to the banks because the targets were so far above the water. When the boat crews elevated their guns to fire at the tops of the banks, the balls went over anyone near the edge of the bank and landed far inland. So long as the river was narrow, the boats could not get far enough away to achieve the line of fire needed to hit men and artillery located on the banks. In the case of wooden boats, such as *Undine* and *Key West*, the ten-pounder guns included in Forrest's artillery were quite capable of disabling the boats in an exchange of gunfire.

THE JOHNSONVILLE RAID

On October 16, 1864, Kelley led Rucker's Brigade out on the road toward Corinth. Rucker was still recovering from wounds, and being placed in command of the brigade was a mark of the confidence Forrest felt in Kelley. The two also enjoyed each other's company because, on this march as on so many others, Forrest and his Escort accompanied the column led by Kelley. The attrition of war was clearly obvious to those who watched the men pass by; the brigade contained only some three hundred men. Even a year earlier, that would have been the size of a regiment. Moving rapidly, the column moved via Purdy and Henderson to Jackson and on to Paris, Tennessee, reaching that town on October 27.[37]

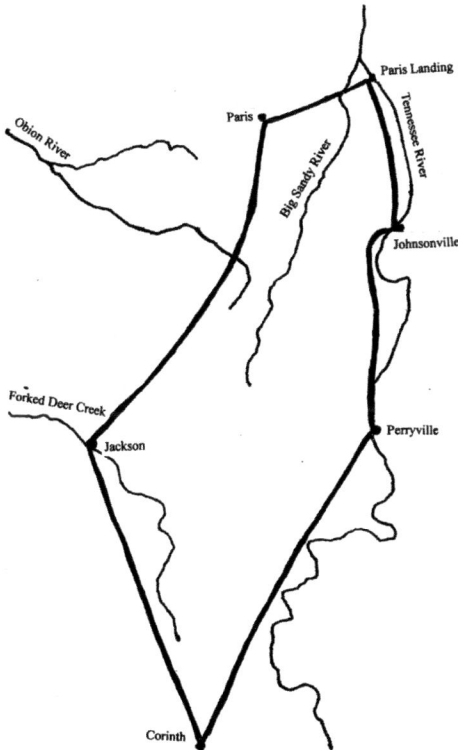

THE JOHNSONVILLE RAID

The Johnsonville raid, where Kelley helped capture a gunboat. *Map by Martha Bradley.*

The motives for this move were, as usual, to damage Union supply lines. John Bell Hood and the Army of Tennessee were already making their move from Georgia toward Tennessee, so Forrest's objective was no longer the supplies going to Sherman's forces. With Hood moving toward Tennessee, the Union garrison in Nashville was now the object of concern for the Confederates. George Thomas was collecting troops from garrisons all over Tennessee and Kentucky to oppose Hood, and Nashville was his secure base, having been in Union hands since February 1862. The well-fortified town contained warehouses full of supplies, yet as the Union force grew, more would be needed. Those supplies came to Nashville along several routes. The Louisville & Nashville Railroad provided a major conduit for supplies, and this road was out of danger from Forrest. He no longer had the men and other resources to penetrate the cordon of defenses along that road. Other supplies reached Nashville via the Cumberland River and from Johnsonville on the Tennessee River. A railroad had been constructed to link Johnsonville with Nashville, and that facility was vulnerable. If Forrest could blockade the Cumberland and Tennessee Rivers, even for a time, the buildup of supplies at Nashville would be hampered. If the supplies at Johnsonville could be destroyed, a temporary shortage might be created. As Forrest moved north to see what he could do along the rivers, he took two pieces of artillery that had no place on an ordinary cavalry raid: 20-pounder guns. The barrel alone of a 20-pounder weighed 1,860 pounds and was eighty-three inches in length. These massive pieces moved so slowly they were not of any real use to cavalry, but they had been sent up from Mobile because of the special nature of what Forrest was attempting.

It should be kept in mind that in the area where Forrest approached the river the Tennessee flows north; thus, downriver is north while upriver is south. To speak of a point as being "below" the Confederate position means that point is to the north, while any point "above" is to the south.

One unit of Confederates under Tyree Bell was put in position at Paris Landing on the Tennessee, while another, under General John Buford, was downstream at the site of Fort Heiman. Kelley moved to the river on October 29, the same day General Rucker returned to duty and resumed command of the brigade. At the river, Kelley found that a transport, the *Venus*, and a gunboat, the familiar foe *Undine*, were trapped between the two Confederate blocking forces but were at a bend in the river out of effective range of both Bell's and Buford's guns. Kelley was sent with his own regiment and that of Colonel Logwood's 15th Tennessee, along with two ten-pounders from Hudson's battery, to take the boats. When an appropriate position was reached on the riverbank, Logwood and the guns took on *Undine* while Kelley placed riflemen to shoot up *Venus* and the U.S. infantrymen guarding it. Within a short time, both vessels had been abandoned by crew and defenders and Kelley was sent in a rowboat to take control of both boats. Kelley boarded *Venus*, where he found the pilot and three men still aboard. Placing his cocked pistol at the head of the pilot, Kelley ordered him to steam to *Undine* and make fast a towrope so both vessels could be brought to the Confederate west bank of the river. The inducement offered was sufficient to obtain full cooperation, and soon the Confederates had their own navy afloat on the Tennessee. Kelley's division commander, General Chalmers, would report, "Lt. Col, Kelley, commanding the 26th Battalion Tenn Cavalry, attacked the transport *Venus*, which was defended by a small detachment of Union infantry, so sharply that she surrendered to him, and the gallant colonel, going on board of her with two companions of his battalion, crossed the river, took possession of the gunboat, and brought both safely to the landing."[38]

The capture of *Undine* was no doubt a proud moment, and the capture of a U.S. Navy gunboat by a detachment of cavalry added a footnote to the annals of military history, but it was the capture of transports *Venus*, *J. W. Chessman* and *Mazeppa* that made glad the hearts of Kelley and his men, as well as all the other Johnnie Rebs present. The abundance of supplies and the feasting that accompanied their capture became one of the legends of the war, told and retold at veterans' reunions as long as there were any left to tell it.

Forrest actually used *Undine* and *Venus* as parts of his command for a couple of days before losing both boats to Union gunfire. *Venus* was armed with the cumbersome twenty-pounders that had been foisted on Forrest, and one can only imagine that he, and all those concerned with their management, were glad to see them off the muddy roads and afloat. When the Yankees captured the guns, it is probable that Forrest, who was immensely protective of his artillery, said "good riddance" and went happily on his way.

The Confederate force moved upstream to Johnsonville and made its famous bombardment of the accumulated supplies, burning acres of warehouses to the ground and sinking numbers of barges and three more gunboats. Kelley's command was placed opposite to Reynoldsburg with two guns of Rice's battery, but the cavalry saw no action on November 4. The next day, Kelley and a section of artillery formed the rearguard of the command as Forrest left for his rendezvous with Hood's army in Alabama. With the rest of Rucker's command, Kelley reached the banks of the

Tennessee at Perryville, Tennessee, and managed to get across using some small boats. The river was rising fast, and the rest of Forrest's men could not cross at that point, so Kelley and Rucker moved along the right bank of the river toward Florence, Alabama, while Forrest led the rest of the men farther west to find a road south to Corinth, from which point he could move east to the vicinity of Florence.[39]

Kelley had every reason to feel pleased with his performance, both personally and as a commanding officer. He had been efficient in his exercise of command over Rucker's brigade while Rucker was recovering from wounds; he had been given the public support of General Forrest and of his division commander, Chalmers; and his men had done their duty at all times. However, the grim reality of dwindling resources and manpower could not be ignored. The last "want to have a good time, jine the cavalry" expedition had just ended, and there was little need to expect another. In the face of these facts, Kelley did not waver, nor did his determination to support the cause to the end lessen. Somehow, he felt, the just cause of the South would still succeed. He was going to do all he could to make that happen.

THE GALLANT HOOD OF TEXAS
PLAYS HELL IN TENNESSEE

"The Yellow Rose of Texas" was a favorite song of Confederate soldiers. It had a swinging tune and lyrics open to more than one interpretation. Like all soldiers in all wars, the men created parody versions of the original, and the next weeks were to see the emergence of a new version. By the end of the year, the Army of Tennessee would be a shadow of its former self, its ranks depleted and its command structure wrecked. Forrest's men, including David Kelley, would have passed through the most trying time of their entire lives, and the familiar tune would now carry bitter words:

> *Now I am going southward, for my heart is full of woe,*
> *I'm going back to Georgia, to see my "Uncle Joe."*
> *You can talk about ole Stonewall and sing of General Lee,*
> *But the "Gallant Hood of Texas" played hell in Tennessee.*

Kelley might not have approved the language, but he would have endorsed the sentiment.

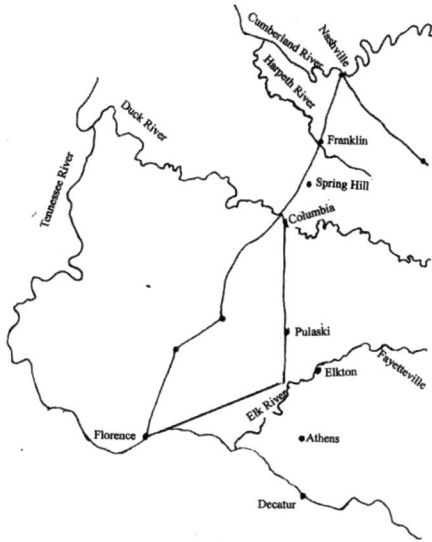

THE NASHVILLE CAMPAIGN

The Nashville Campaign. *Map by Martha Bradley.*

When John Bell Hood and Forrest met at Florence, Alabama, on November 18, 1864, Hood had about twenty-seven thousand infantry and artillerymen with him. He had brought two thousand cavalry with him under General William Jackson. Forrest had about four thousand men with him and would take command of all the cavalry. This gave Hood a force of about thirty-three thousand men. What he was going to do with them is not clear and seems not to have been clear in Hood's own mind. What was clear was that the army needed to move quickly if it were to have any chance at all.

General George Thomas commanded all U.S. troops in the area, and there were plenty of troops to be had. But the men were scattered from St. Louis to Chattanooga to Decatur, Alabama. Thomas had perhaps eight thousand men in Nashville serving as a garrison. General Steedman had some five thousand men in Chattanooga who could be brought to Nashville via the Nashville & Chattanooga Railroad. As Steedman moved toward Nashville, he could pick up some five thousand men from garrisons in such places as Tullahoma and another four thousand in Murfreesboro. General Schofield commanded two army corps, the 4th and the 23rd, which contained about twenty-two thousand men. These were positioned in northern Alabama and in southern middle Tennessee. A.J. Smith had another army corps coming to aid Thomas but it was in St. Louis waiting on boats to carry it to Nashville. Wilson commanded some ten thousand cavalrymen, although several thousand were dismounted for lack of horses.

This disposition of forces means Hood had a chance to wreak havoc if he moved swiftly. There was a good chance of defeating part of Schofield's command, cutting the railroad from Decatur, isolating the Union troops there, moving toward Tullahoma to cut off the Yankees there and also isolating Steedman in Chattanooga. Then attention could be given to the garrison in Murfreesboro before moving toward Nashville. The possibility of winning an important victory was faint, but it was possible if everything went right. It did not.

Because of the need to shoe horses and the necessity of waiting for rations to arrive from Mississippi, the Army of Tennessee stayed at Florence until November 21. Only then did Forrest send his three divisions north over a wide front. Chalmers's division, of which Kelley was a part, followed the old Military Road, first used by Andrew Jackson in the War of 1812, toward Lawrenceburg. Almost immediately, contact was made with elements of the 6th U.S. Cavalry Division under Colonel Horace Capron. Daily skirmishing marked Kelley's advance, and darkness did not necessarily bring an end to the fight. Forrest was in a hurry to reach the crossings of the Duck River at Columbia, Tennessee. At that point he could cut the Tennessee & Alabama Railroad, isolating the Union garrison at Decatur, and also slow or block the retreat of Schofield's force as it moved toward Nashville. Schofield was anxious to get across the Duck but wanted to make a stand on the north side to buy time for the scattered U.S. forces to reach Nashville.

At Fouche Springs on November 23 the cavalry forces collided in a more forceful fashion. Rucker, with Forrest personally present, was pressing Capron toward Columbia. The divisions of Buford and Jackson had moved toward Pulaski in an attempt to cut off the rest of Wilson's cavalry. Darkness was falling, and Forrest was riding ahead of the main column, accompanied by his Escort and Kelley's command. Because of the weather, most of the men were wearing oilcloths. In the gloom of falling night, Forrest and the Escort rode into the head of a Federal column and a fracas erupted, with Forrest's adjutant, Major Strange, knocking aside a pistol pressed to Forrest's head an instant before it was fired. When the Union column retreated, Forrest followed, sending back word to Rucker to bring up the rest of his brigade. Kelley was sent around the left while Forrest and the Escort went to the right, both groups intending to get in the rear of the Yankees, and Rucker was to charge up the middle to take them in front. Kelley was not able to get into position before Forrest made contact with the Union rear, and desperate, confused fighting broke out. Just then Rucker charged home and Kelley made contact, and the entire Union force left in great haste for Mount Pleasant, where they paused briefly before moving for Columbia. The pause at Mount Pleasant was long enough for Rucker to catch up with them and capture thirty-five thousand rounds of small arms ammunition and the guard that had been left with it.[40]

On the evening of the next day, November 24, Kelley reached the vicinity of Columbia and, with the rest of Chalmers's command, surrounded the town on three sides, with the Duck River being on the fourth. Since the town was occupied by the U.S. 4th and 23rd Army Corps, plus Hatch's cavalry division—some thirty thousand men—the best the Southern cavalry could do was to harass the U.S. troops and wait for the Confederate foot soldiers to come up. Kelley played a role in this by supporting the artillery whose fire kept the Union infantry from advancing outside their breastworks.[41] From November 25th through 27, there was indecisive skirmishing around Columbia. During the night of the twenty-seventh/twenty-eighth, Schofield pulled his men back to the north bank of the Duck River, and Kelley was part of the outflanking column that crossed the river at Carr's Mill some seven miles upstream from Columbia. On the night of the twenty-eighth, Kelley was near Spring Hill and was engaged in the fighting around that town on the twenty-ninth. The men of the 3rd Tennessee did not play a prominent role in that confused engagement, although they fought hard enough to exhaust all their ammunition and were forced to request a resupply from a nearby infantry ordnance train. When the U.S. Army was found, the next morning, to have passed the Confederate position during the night, Kelley was sent up the Carter's Creek Pike toward Franklin. During the infantry attack at Franklin, Kelley and his men were posted on the left of the Confederate line and escaped the fiercest of the fighting. On December 1, Kelley was part of the cavalry pursuit that moved up the Hillsboro Pike while the main infantry force moved up the Franklin-Nashville Pike.[42]

As the battered ranks of the Army of Tennessee reached Nashville, they were placed in position along hills facing the Union-occupied fortifications. Both armies held semicircular positions with the flanks resting on the Cumberland River both above and below Nashville. The U.S. line was shorter and was anchored at regular intervals by massive earthworks that had been under construction since 1862. The reinforcements under A.J. Smith had begun arriving the night of November 30, and Steedman had brought most of his troops in from Chattanooga on December 1. Thomas had so many troops on hand that he decided to leave eight thousand to hold Murfreesboro, which was protected by the sprawling earthwork known as Fortress Rosecrans.

Hood's line was longer and more thinly manned. The Confederate right was held by Cheatham's Corps, with the flank resting on Brown's Creek, but a gap of two miles lay between the creek and the Cumberland. This gap was filled by a thin cavalry screen. The men of S.D. Lee held the center of the line while A.P. Stewart's Corps held the left flank, terminating on the Hillsboro Pike. The flank of the infantry line was refused, and five detached redoubts were begun to provide a more secure anchor for the bent-back portion of the line. For eight miles between the Hillsboro Pike and the Cumberland, there was only the cavalry division of Chalmers, some 1,200 men in all.[43]

Chalmers knew that the Cumberland was a vital supply route for Thomas's army, and he moved to block it. Kelley, the experienced gunboat fighter, was sent with his regiment of about three hundred men and two ten-pounder guns from Rice's Battery to set up a blockade at a bend in the river on the south bank directly across from Bell's Landing and Bell's Mill. This location is today called Kelley's Point.[44] Kelley positioned his guns on high ground near the river where it would be difficult for gunboats to elevate their cannon sufficiently to hit his position. The cavalrymen were scattered along the banks, under cover, to pepper any targets with rifle fire. Soon two transports, *Prairie State* and *Prima Donna*, came upriver, and Lieutenant H.H. Briggs took them under fire with the artillery under his command. The two boats put into shore and surrendered, leaving Kelley with fifty-six prisoners, 179 horses and mules and a great deal of grain in sacks. The boats were taken a short distance downstream and unloaded.[45]

The senior naval officer in Nashville was Lieutenant Commander Le Roy Fitch, a veteran of several campaigns on the western rivers. Fitch had just arrived in Nashville as the commander of the boats protecting the transports bringing General A.J. Smith's corps to reinforce Thomas. Under Fitch's command were the USS *Carondelet*, one of the Eads ironclads built in 1861, mounting fourteen guns; the USS *Neosho*, a river monitor commissioned in 1863 and a veteran of the Red Rive campaign; and USS *Moose*, Fitch's flagboat, a wooden stern wheeler built in 1863 and lightly armored so as to be called a "tinclad." Fitch also had under his command *Peosta*, *Fairplay*, *Silver Lake*, *Brilliant*, *Springfield*, *Reindeer* and *Victory*, altogether the largest fleet to see service on the Cumberland at any time during the war.[46] Fitch knew he needed to try to reopen the river to travel and he needed to recapture the two transports to prevent the Confederates from using them to cross cavalry to the north side of the river where lay the Louisville & Nashville Railroad, the main lifeline of Thomas's force. Unknown to Fitch, Kelley had been reinforced by two more guns, twelve-pounder howitzers, and he had created two artillery positions.

During the night of December 4–5, Fitch moved downstream with *Carondelet, Fairplay, Moose, Reindeer* and *Silver Lake*. About 12:45 a.m., *Carondelet* came abreast of the known Confederate position and opened fire. Darkness had allowed the ship to approach unobserved, but Kelley soon opened return fire. *Carondelet* steamed back and forth in front of the Confederate artillery, keeping the guns under fire, while *Fairplay* continued down the river to recapture the two transports. These were soon in flames, and *Fairplay* started back for Nashville. Meanwhile, *Moose* had moved into the zone of fire and had come to a halt so as to allow *Carondelet* room to maneuver. The engagement lasted about ninety minutes and ended with the naval force returning to Nashville and Kelley sending for a resupply of ammunition.[47]

On December 6, Fitch made another effort. Gathering a fleet of transports that needed to go downriver, the lieutenant commander put *Neosho* and *Carondelet* in the lead, followed by the tinclads and timberclads. Since *Neosho* was the most stoutly armored and the heaviest armed, it was decided that it would confront Kelley's artillery positions while *Carondelet* fired from a distance and the other vessels stayed out of the way. Before noon, the battle was joined. Heavy naval guns bellowed and smoke billowed, and the Confederate artillery replied. *Neosho* was struck more than one hundred times, and all the lightly protected external features of the monitor—lifeboats, unarmored pilothouse, flagstaff, etc.—were destroyed. The "fighting" pilothouse was so covered by wreckage that the officers stationed there could not see well enough to steer the boat, and *Neosho* finally fell back to clear away the tangle. An inspection showed that Kelley had come very close to winning a major victory. A ten-pound shell had penetrated the magazine of *Neosho* but had failed to explode—a telling commentary on the quality of ordnance supplied to the Confederate forces. Darkness put an end to the artillery duel with no lives lost on either side. This fight would live for years in Kelley's memory. In 1896, while he was pastor of the Methodist church in Columbia, Tennessee, he wrote an article for the *Confederate Veteran* in which he asked that the man who commanded the two Parrott guns contact him, if the gunner were still alive.[48]

The weather was about to become the focal point of attention for all the soldiers gathered in and around Nashville. About noon on December 7, a sudden squall of wind and rain marked a frontal passage. By morning on December 8, the ground was frozen, and the next day rain began to fall, freezing as it touched the ground. Soon all surfaces were covered with two to three inches of ice that was topped with sleet and snow. This ice storm put an end to all major military movements. Despite the weather, Hood was focusing on events at Murfreesboro. He seems to have been convinced that either the Murfreesboro garrison would attempt to break through to Nashville or that Thomas would detach additional men to reinforce the troops at Murfreesboro. To counter either of these moves, Hood sent an order on December 10 for Chalmers to detach the brigade commanded by Biffle to move from the left all the way over to the right flank and help plug the gap between Cheatham's infantry lines and the Cumberland River. This left only Rucker's Brigade on the left flank, so Ector's brigade of infantry was sent over to the Harding Pike. This "brigade" was smaller than a full-strength regiment, having fewer than seven hundred men in its ranks.[49]

December 14 brought warmer weather, and the ice began to melt rapidly. On both sides of the lines, the military implications of the break in the weather were obvious. On the morning of December 15, Thomas struck against both flanks of the Confederate line, although his main thrust was to the west and then south against the Confederate left. The line stretched from the Tennessee & Alabama Railroad, near Murfreesboro Pike, across to Hillsboro Pike, where the infantry position was refused and protected by a line of small, detached redoubts. From Hillsboro Pike, there was a gap of over two miles to the Harding Pike, where Ector's brigade was in position, and beyond that another gap to the Charlotte Pike, where Chalmers had his cavalry. On the Confederate right, Steedman brought his Union troops up to attack Cheatham's flank but the troops, many of them members of the USCT, walked into a trap when they marched up to a deep railroad cut and could not get across to assault the Confederate lines on the other side. On the Confederate left, Ector's tiny infantry force found itself facing the army corps of Wagner and A.J. Smith and rapidly fell back until they could find a crossroads leading to the main Confederate line along the Hillsboro Pike. The 6th U.S. Cavalry Division moved toward Kelley's position on the Cumberland, but Kelley had left the place during the night of December 14–15 and was miles away by the time the first Union dismounted troopers reached his old position. Falling back toward Harding Pike, the Confederate cavalrymen put up such resistance as they could, but their primary focus was to escape cross-country to regain contact with the main line. During much of the day, Kelley was in field command of Rucker's brigade, as Rucker tried to get instructions as to where and how to make an effective stand. For much of the time, the brigade numbered only five hundred men, the rest being scattered among picket posts and scouting duty.[50]

Fighting started along the Hillsboro Pike at about the same time the cavalry began to skirmish in the area along Harding and Charlotte Pikes. The refused line of detached redoubts came under attack by dismounted cavalrymen from Wilson's Corps under the direct command of Colonel Datus Coon. The first of these, Redoubt #5, fell quickly. Captain Charles Lumsden, a graduate of Virginia Military Institute, commanding four guns and about 150 infantry, more stoutly defended the next in line, #4. This position held off four batteries and two entire brigades for more than three hours. The eventual fall of Redoubt #4 brought the infantry along Hillsboro Pike, sheltered behind a stone wall, under fire, and a Union division commanded by Brigadier John McArthur attacked the "hinge" where the refused portion of the line bent to meet the main part of the position. The successful attack on the hinge flanked the main Confederate position and forced the entire line to fall back. As the Confederates fell back, some of them in disorder, Kelley led his cavalrymen up to the line of the Hillsboro Pike. Kelley had been moving gradually farther and farther south in an attempt to get around the flank of the Union attack troops so he could rejoin the main Confederate line. He led his men across the pike several hundred yards beyond the right end of Wilson's line of dismounted men, and when Wilson saw them, he became fearful of being flanked in his turn and halted his assault. This fortuitous coincidence gave the Confederates a chance to fall back to their secondary position and make a stand. Darkness fell just about this time and also aided the retreat.[51]

The new Confederate line stretched from Peach Orchard Hill just east of the Franklin Pike to Shy's Hill just east of the Hillsboro Pike. Granny White Pike is between Franklin Pike and Shy's Hill but is closer to the Shy's Hill than to Peach Orchard Hill. Shy's Hill did not have a name at the time of the battle.

The second day of the battle was quiet and calm for much of the day. On the Confederate right, as on the first day, there was an abortive assault on the fortifications on Peach Orchard Hill, and like the first day, soldiers of the USCT made this attack. All during the morning hours, Wilson was slowly probing the extreme left flank of the Confederate line, and about noon, he succeeded in getting about four thousand dismounted men in the rear of that flank. The infantry commander, General Schofield, was hesitant to commit his 23rd Corps to an attack, and this gave the Confederates an opportunity to counter Wilson's move. Kelley and the 3rd Tennessee were sent to the top of a steep hill to the south and east of Shy's Hill to block the move of Wilson's men. They skirmished there for about an hour until a strong attack by men under Colonel Datus Coon dislodged them, with Kelley losing some seventy-five men captured. As Kelley led his battered survivors down the northern slopes, he met Ector's brigade coming to his rescue. The two forces charged together back up the hill, retaking the prisoners and reestablishing Kelley's former position. This lasted until General Edward Hatch came up with large Union reinforcements, including artillery. This time, Kelley led his men off the hill and turned to the east to protect the approaches to the Granny White Pike. This was about 3:15 p.m., and the shadows were getting long as the sun sank toward the west.[52]

About 4:00 p.m., Brigadier John McArthur decided that someone in the U.S. Army ought to attack and see if the partial victory won on December 15 could not be made complete on December 16. Without approval from any higher headquarters, he sent his troops forward to assault Shy's Hill. As his men went up the slopes of the hill, others to the east made a move against the Confederate line where it crossed Granny White Pike. To the great surprise of all concerned, the Southern line crumbled, and the gray soldiers began to run.

Kelley had just gotten his men into position to guard the western approaches to Granny White Pike after falling back from their hill. He quickly readjusted his lines so that some of his men faced north, up the pike, in the direction from which the Confederate infantry were running, while the rest of his men continued to face west to counter the approaching Union troops in that area.

Rucker had left his command in Kelley's hands after they reached Granny White Pike and had gone to see if he could get any clear idea of the circumstances from an infantry commander. While Rucker was absent, the thin line was struck by Union cavalrymen under Edward Hatch, John Croxton and J.H. Hammond. Kelley worked furiously to hold his men to the work. One participant in the fight described him as riding back and forth along the battle line, constantly calling on the men to "pour it on 'em." As a Methodist minister, Kelley had to be somewhat selective in the language he used to encourage the men, even in this emergency. Rucker returned in the midst of the turmoil and was soon wounded and captured. As darkness made the fight even more confused, Kelley managed to disentangle his men from the Yankees and to lead them across country to the Franklin Pike. There the remnants of S.D. Lee's Corps were making a stand as a rearguard.[53]

The fierce stand put up by Kelley took a heavy toll on his men, but it also convinced the Union cavalry not to push too hard on the next day. The

Confederates fell back to Franklin, hastily destroying the bridges over the Harpeth River, and then took up the road toward Spring Hill and Columbia. Kelley and the remnants of Chalmers Brigade "fought every day protecting the rear of General Hood's army until it had crossed Rutherford Creek." Forrest was not present at the Battle of Nashville, having been sent with most of the cavalry to contain the Union garrison at Murfreesboro. As soon as he reached the army, Forrest took over the rearguard action. Kelley saw action at Richland Creek, north of Pulaski; was in reserve at Anthony's Hill; and was again in reserve at Sugar Creek. Kelley gladly crossed the Tennessee River on December 27 and hoped for a little rest.[54]

The Final Days of the War

As soon as the cavalry had crossed the Tennessee, Forrest left Roddy to watch north Alabama and established his headquarters at Corinth, Mississippi. All the troops whose homes were still in Confederate lines were sent home to see if they could acquire fresh horses. They certainly could get new clothes and, with luck, could convince others to return when they did. This welcome respite did not come to Kelley and his men from middle Tennessee. They, along with many others who could not go home again, were sent to Okolona, where food and forage were relatively plentiful. This was not a time of uninterrupted rest and replenishment, however, for numerous scouts and small expeditions were sent out to harass the enemy. Forrest also decided to reorganize his force into three divisions and to consolidate the numerous small regiments so as to make his corps a more effective fighting unit. In this reorganization, all the Mississippi regiments were assigned to General Chalmers, the men from Alabama and Kentucky were to be commanded by Buford and W.H. Jackson got the Tennessee and Texas troops. This move would give Kelley a new division and brigade commander. For reasons unknown, during this reorganization Kelley signed an oath of loyalty to the Confederacy. It stated:

I, David C. Kelley, age 37 years, 2 months, born in Wilson County Tennessee, appointed from 3rd day of April 1862, so solemnly swear or affirm that while I continue in the service I will bear true faith and yield obedience to the Confederate States of America, and that I will serve them honestly and faithfully against their enemies, and that I will observe and obey the orders of the President of the Confederate Sates, and the orders of the Officers appointed over me, according to the Rules and Articles of War.[55]

W.H. Jackson was no stranger to Kelley, as Jackson had served with Forrest for a considerable period. The new brigade commander would be a different story. Tyree Bell was selected to command one brigade in the new Tennessee division, but the 3rd Tennessee was not assigned to that veteran officer. After waiting for a few weeks, Forrest named Alexander William Campbell to command the rest of the Tennessee troops. Campbell was the former colonel of the 33rd Tennessee Infantry and had been severely wounded at Shiloh. Returning from medical leave, Campbell had served as inspector general to Lieutenant General Polk and then worked with the conscript bureau under Gideon Pillow. While on a mission behind Union lines, Campbell was captured at Lexington, Tennessee, in 1863 and was not exchanged until February 1865. At that point, he became inspector general on Forrest's staff, from which position he was chosen to command a brigade. Kelley was a distant relative of Alexander Campbell through his mother's family.[56] Perhaps the chaotic conditions prevailing in the closing days of the war are responsible, but for some reason Campbell did not file reports about the activities of his brigade, so there is no detailed information about Kelley and the 3rd Tennessee for this period. The records do show that Jackson had about 3,200 men in his entire division.[57]

On March 22, 1865, the Union cavalry under Wilson left the vicinity of Waterloo, Alabama. This expedition moved south in three columns through Jasper to Elyton, a place now named Birmingham. On March 26, Jackson's division received orders to move to Pickensville, Alabama, and from there to march to Tuscaloosa and on to Selma, the important Confederate arsenal on the Alabama River. Jackson reached Tuscaloosa about noon on March 30, the same day a Union brigade commanded by Croxton left Elyton for the same location. Jackson and Tyree Bell lingered in Tuscaloosa for a dinner at the home of John Blocker, a prominent plantation owner, while their troops, presumably under the command of Campbell, marched toward Centerville and a significant river crossing.

During the morning of March 31, the Union cavalry coming from Elyton struck at right angles the road from Tuscaloosa to Centerville. When the Yankees reached the road, they could see that troops had recently passed toward Centerville, so they turned in that direction to follow. Unknown to them, the Union brigade of 1,800 men had entered a four-mile-long gap in the Confederate line of march. All the Confederate cavalry was in their front, and in their rear came Morton's battery and the supply wagons. During the night of March 31–April 1, Bell discovered this state of affairs and offered a Forrest-like plan of action. Bell would lead his men by secondary roads to gain the rear of the Union troops while Campbell remained in their front. When Bell attacked from the rear, Campbell would charge in front. Jackson accepted this plan, and Bell took to the road. By this time, the Union riders had turned back toward Tuscaloosa but had themselves gone off on a side road, missing Morton's battery and the supply wagons. Late in the morning, Bell hit the Union column and began to drive them toward the Black Warrior River. Campbell did not make contact.[58]

On April 1, couriers carrying messages between Forrest and Jackson were captured. With the information so acquired, Wilson was able to deploy his forces so as to prevent a Confederate concentration at Selma and so was able to win an easy victory there. Forrest took his men north and west of Selma following the loss of the town, while Wilson moved on toward Montgomery. By April 4, Jackson had reached Forrest's lines at Marion, Alabama, and a strange interlude began. The Confederates had come into a pocket of country that had escaped the worst ravages of the war, but the population was fierce in its devotion to the Confederate cause. The outpouring of support, including food and clothes, was reminiscent of the early days of the war. But all knew the war was over and they had lost. On several occasions during this interval, veterans remember Kelley preaching to their command.

On April 30, General Richard Taylor, commander of the entire theater, agreed to a truce with General Canby of the U.S. forces. On May 4, terms of surrender were agreed to, and the next day these terms were announced to Forrest's men. May 8 saw the men fall into formation for the last time. There were no parades, no lines of bluecoats through which the men had to march, no Yankee presence at all; the men fell in and passed over their weapons to their own brigade ordnance officers. On May 9, Forrest published his "Farewell Address," and the next day a handful of U.S. Army officers turned up to countersign paroles so Forrest's command could start for home. Kelley's oath stated:

I, the undersigned Prisoner of War, belonging to the Army of the Department of Alabama, Mississippi, and East Louisiana, having been surrendered by Lt. Gen. R. Taylor, CSA, Commanding said Department to Maj. Gen E.R.S. Canby USA commanding Army and district of West Mississippi, do hereby give my solemn parole of honor that I will not hereafter serve in the Armies of the Confederate States or in any military capacity act against the United States of America or render aid to the enemies of the same until properly exchanged in such manner as shall be mutually approved by the respective authorities. Sworn at Gainesville, Alabama, this 11th day of May 1865.

*The above named officer will not be disturbed by United States authorities
as long as he observes his parole and the laws in force where he resides.*

W.H. Jackson approved the document for the Confederacy, and Brigadier General E.S. Dennis signed for the United States.[59]

David C. Kelley, man of war, had become once again a man of peace.

Chapter 4

God's Warrior

A New Beginning

As David Kelley rode north from Gainesville, Alabama, he had much on his mind. He had a wife and three children he had not seen for many months. How he was to support them was a puzzle. Kelley was a minister and intended to pursue that profession, but the Methodist Episcopal Church, South, was in total disarray. The physical property of the church had been confiscated during the war by the authority of the United States government, with the buildings turned over to the Northern Methodist Church. Across the South, many churches were physically occupied by pastors from the North whom the Southern congregations refused to support either by attending their services or giving to pay their salaries. This problem would not soon be solved. In 1879, fourteen years after the end of the war, the *New York Christian Advocate* published an article declaring: "We claim the South, because the republic which we have recently saved by Methodist conscience and Methodist bayonets now demands at our hands another salvation by Methodist ideas and faith. Nothing is gained by shutting our eyes to the fact, that the preservation of the Union and the reign of moral law all over the South depends more on what is done by our church than upon any other force."[1] In short, a spirit of self-righteousness saw the South as morally bankrupt, and only the virtuous Yankees could save the land. Reconciliation was not just a matter of convincing the South to accept the results of the war; the South was going to be required to accept Yankee moral superiority.

Even if Kelley could find a congregation with a building, how would the people pay the preacher? The economy of the South was devastated, and the rival plans for Reconstruction promoted by Lincoln (now advocated by Johnson) and Congress did not include any provisions for restoring the economy. The simple business of survival would be a challenge for some time to come.

Less prominent in Kelley's thinking, but not absent from his concerns, were his lifelong interests in education and missions. How could these be pursued without money or any other resources?

There was also the matter of readjusting to life as a minister. Kelley had always been a man under discipline, as a missionary, as a pastor and as a Confederate officer. But he had served under Bedford Forrest, and that experience had shown him that rank and good sense did not always go together. Kelley knew quite well that many of the clashes Forrest had had with higher-ranking officers had been disputes between common sense on Forrest's part and a lack of comprehending the situation on the part of the superior. Now Kelley would find himself dealing with a church hierarchy in which promotion to high rank often had more to do with personal connections than it did with demonstrated ability to plan, lead and execute. Kelley might be once more God's warrior, but he would still be a Rebel! For the rest of his life, he would find himself periodically at odds with the official stance of the Methodist Episcopal Church, South, and he would frequently find himself opposing the views of his bishop. Kelley did not shrink from the religious fray any more than he had done from the physical combat of the battlefield.

Huntsville, Alabama, had been Kelley's last pastoral assignment before the war. There had been no meeting of the Tennessee Methodist Conference in 1864 and none so far in 1865. Huntsville was part of the Tennessee Conference, but the church there was in ruins. The United States garrison troops had used the sanctuary of the church building for a barracks, and the basement, which was flush with the ground on one side, had provided the troops with a stable. A carelessly tended fire in the part used as a barracks had spread to the entire structure, and nothing was left. With his wife and family in Wilson County, Tennessee, where both David and Manerva had relatives, he rode to that location.

Sometime in the summer of 1865, Kelley was assigned to the Lebanon Station. This meant he was responsible for holding services and overseeing the business affairs of the Methodist church in the town of Lebanon, Tennessee, and in several surrounding rural churches. This was a genuine homecoming for Kelley, since he had been born at Leeville, just outside Lebanon; his father had founded the Methodist church at that village; Kelley had been baptized there and had met his wife there; and his father was buried there. Laying aside his saber and pistols, Kelley became once more God's warrior.

Despite the obstacles facing them, the Methodist churches of Wilson County thrived under Kelley's ministrations. Kelley was able to support his wife, Manerva, and their three children, Lizzie Mannie (Daisy), John Harris and Elizabeth. By 1867, several of the rural churches had pastors, many of them men who farmed during the week and preached on Sunday, but still, there was a man on site to do all the things necessary for a church to function, preaching being the least of these duties. That year, Kelley became presiding elder, preaching at the church in Lebanon and providing supervision for the work of the men at the smaller churches. Kelley also took a hand in reopening the Corona Female Academy, acting as president of the school. This proved to be a daunting task in the weak economy, and the school closed after only one year.

The year 1868 was a time of triumph and tragedy for David Kelley. Cumberland College (now Cumberland University) had reopened its doors in Lebanon, and in recognition of Kelley's devotion to education and his work in the community, the college awarded him the honorary degree of doctor of divinity (DD) at its June commencement ceremonies. The tragedy was the death of Manerva, Kelley's wife of fourteen years, and another child. Kelley did not publish any memoirs, but his daughter, Mannie, wrote a memoir in 1880 that said the child was a daughter named Josephine and that her mother, Manerva, died of a hemorrhage accompanying childbirth. The tombstone erected by David in Cedar Grove Cemetery in Lebanon, Tennessee, shows a mother holding a baby in her arms, and the epitaph says: "Two Babes Went to Heaven Before She Died, A Third Now Lies at the Mother's Side." One baby had been born to the couple while they were in China, a daughter named Mimi. She lived just over a year, dying on the trip back to the United States, and was buried at sea. On their return from China, another child was born just after the couple landed in Richmond and was either still-born or lived only a matter of hours. No name has been found. That child was buried in Richmond. Now the grieving widower, with three young children, accepted an appointment to the Tulip Street Methodist Church in Nashville.

Perhaps it was the prospect of a fresh start surrounded by new scenes and new people where every tree and hill did not remind him of his lost wife that attracted Kelley to Nashville. At any rate, for the next forty years, until his death in 1909, his life would be intertwined with Nashville. For only

Mannie's grave. The inscription reads: "Two Babes Went to Heaven Before She Died, A Third Now Lies at the Mother's Side."

three of these years would he be outside the town or its suburbs, and his greatest accomplishments in the service of the church and its God would be in Nashville. There would also be occasions when Kelley kicked over the ecclesiastical traces, showing that he was a Rebel yet, although he served a different commander.

Kelley also found a new partner for his life in Nashville. On January 14, 1869, he married a distant cousin, Mary Owen Campbell. Together they would have four children and share their lives for some twenty years. Mary Owen Campbell was the oldest daughter of William Bowen Campbell, a man who had been prominent in politics in Tennessee for many years, having served as congressman for three terms on the Whig ticket and as governor from 1851 to 1853 representing the same ticket. Opposed to secession, Campbell had been appointed a brigadier in the U.S. Army by President Lincoln, but he served in that capacity for only a brief time. In 1866, Campbell was returned to Congress as a Democrat, but he died in 1867.

The addition to the family of a stepmother, and an eventual blending of half brothers and sisters, was not always easy. Lizzie Mannie, known as

Daisy, was the oldest child when David married Mary Owen Campbell, and she seemed to remain somewhat distant from her new mother. David's mother, now a widow, provided all the help she could, frequently caring for the children at Itinerant's Rest when yellow fever or other illness broke out in Nashville. On occasion Mary Owen joined the children, even though the country was not to her liking.[2]

Kelley was pastor at Tulip Street for one year, becoming pastor of the preeminent Methodist church in Nashville, the McKendree Church, in 1870. He would keep this pastorate until 1879. For part of his tenure he was also presiding elder for Nashville. McKendree was a good congregation for Kelley to lead. The members of the church, like Kelley, held progressive views on many issues, including personal behavior. Following the war, urban Methodists generally dropped the antebellum restrictions concerning clothing styles, wearing jewelry and types of entertainment judged appropriate for church members. In rural areas, the old standards of personal deportment continued to have many adherents, so the Methodist Episcopal Church, South, experienced something of a town-country split. Kelley was quite at home in the town.[3] His critics would sometimes call Kelley "the pet of the fashionable Methodists," but he was a clever, powerful speaker and possessed a lively and probing mind. As such, he was quite capable of sticking a pin in the balloon of pomposity displayed by opponents. He would also become a thorn in the side of those who advocated a strict orthodoxy, including several Methodist bishops.[4]

Even before moving to Nashville, Kelley had come under the supervision of Bishop Holland N. McTyeire. The two men were not strangers. For several years prior to the war, McTyeire had been the editor of the *Christian Advocate*, the Methodist paper that circulated in middle Tennessee and north Alabama. McTyeire had been a staunch defender of slavery, arguing in editorials that the institution had both a biblical basis and divine approval. When the sectional debate grew hotter, McTyeire advocated secession as the best way of avoiding contamination by Northern Unitarian ideas and as a protection against domestic terrorists such as John Brown. After the U.S. Army occupied Nashville in February 1862, McTyeire went to southern Alabama, where he spent the rest of the war as pastor of several churches. He had been named bishop for middle Tennessee in 1867 and took up his residence on South High Street (today's Sixth Avenue) just a short distance from the McKendree Church.[5]

In addition to both men having been staunch Confederates, they shared an interest in education, though they would have sharp disagreements as to what type of education was appropriate for ministers. The issue was whether the Methodist Church should support a university that gave all students, including prospective ministers, a broad liberal arts education and advance training in some specialized areas (Kelley's idea) or whether the church should establish a school whose primary task was to train Methodist preachers (McTyeire's view).

FOUNDING VANDERBILT UNIVERSITY

In a series of articles published in the *Christian Advocate* in the summer of 1867, Kelley argued for a trained ministry for the Methodist Church. He wanted candidates for the ministry to have theological training, but he also wanted them taught the principles of critical thinking, using the liberal arts as the basis for this teaching. This was not a universally popular view in the Methodist Episcopal Church, South. In 1870, the General Conference of the church passed a resolution against theological studies and in favor of less complex biblical studies conducted at the college level.[6] Theological training includes study in philosophy, the historical development of doctrine, ancient languages, the evolution of biblical texts and the history of the church. Biblical studies focus on the content of the books of the Bible and do not usually require pupils to know Hebrew or Greek to read the Bible in its original languages.

Undaunted by the resolution passed by the 1870 General Conference, a three-part series appeared in the *Christian Advocate* written by "Progress," almost certainly Kelley. These articles called for a great university that would include a department of theology. This proposed university was intended to rival the well-known schools in New England. As the 1871 Tennessee General Conference was preparing to meet in Lebanon, two editorials by W.C. Johnson, along with several letters supporting the views expressed, were published in the *Western Methodist* calling for four Methodist conferences to cooperate in founding a "great, central university." The north Alabama, Memphis, north Mississippi and Tennessee conferences were called on to choose a single location for such an institution and then to pool their resources to endow it.[7] Such a plan would kill some existing colleges that were struggling to recover from the effects of the war. Wesleyan College at Florence, Alabama, was one of these, but pooling scarce resources was an appealing argument.

Kelley knew the *Western Methodist* had published the proposal and that it had strong support, so when the Tennessee Conference met, he

Old Central, Vanderbilt University. Kelley took notes at many meetings of the University Board of Trust.

put on the floor a motion to establish a committee to investigate the idea. The motion was adopted, and in 1872, delegates from Memphis, middle Tennessee, Alabama, Mississippi, Louisiana and Arkansas met in Memphis. Bishop McTyeire moved that the church proceed to found a university that would include a theological school to supply ministers for the church. Kelley supported the motion and was named to the twenty-four-member Board of Trustees. At the first meeting of the board, Kelley was elected secretary, a post he would hold for thirty years.[8] As secretary, Kelley was also a member of the Executive Committee of the Board. Serving with him were Judge Edward H. East of Nashville, president; Alexander Little Page Green, treasurer; and four others. This group was given the responsibilities of preparing a charter for the university, securing the approval of the College of Bishops and beginning a fund drive to raise $1 million.[9]

Kelley wrote a formal paper for the consideration of the bishops, calling on them to support the university. When the College of Bishops met to consider the paper, considerable opposition was voiced, and the college turned down Kelley's appeal. As a result, there was never a strong, formal bond established between the university and the Methodist Church.[10]

Bishop McTyeire led the fundraising effort. In 1873, the bishop went to New York City for surgery. He had another objective in mind as well. In 1869, Cornelius Vanderbilt, age seventy-three, married Frank Armstrong Crawford, age thirty. Frank owed her unusual name to a promise her father had given his business partner that the first child in his family would be named for the partner. The first child was a girl, but the promise was kept. Frank was a cousin of the wife of Bishop McTyeire. As a relative who held a respectable position, Bishop McTyeire was invited to convalesce in the Vanderbilt mansion.[11] Cornelius Vanderbilt had no qualms about associating with such a virulent Rebel as McTyeire. Not only had he married a woman who had nursed wounded Confederates, the "Commodore" had been one of the Northern businessmen who had put up the bail money to have Jefferson Davis released from Federal custody. McTyeire knew Vanderbilt did not like to be asked for money, so he did not ask. Instead, in conversations after dinner, the bishop described the plans for the university, and on his last night in New York, Vanderbilt offered to endow the university. On March 26, 1873, the Board of Trust met at McKendree Methodist Church and formally received the gift.[12]

This is the greatest contribution to education, and the most sterling accomplishment of his career, for David Kelley. His interest in education had helped to found a major university.

EDUCATION FOR THE FREEDMEN

Kelley had always been concerned for African Americans who were part of the Methodist Church or who came into its sphere of influence. Before the war, there had been over 200,000 black members of the Methodist Episcopal Church, South, worshiping in the same building as the white members of the church. At the end of the war, these black members departed in droves, mostly for the CME (originally Colored Methodist Episcopal Church, now the Christian Methodist Episcopal Church) founded in Jackson, Tennessee, in 1870. This separate organization was created with the full support of the white Methodist Church in the South. Kelley was one of the church leaders who publicly commended the move.

While Kelley said "goodbye," he did not say "good riddance." He felt that the church universal would not prosper unless all its branches did well, so Kelley maintained contact with the leaders of the new church body and urged white churches to support education for the ministers of the new denomination. That education would have to come through private schools.

In the early days of Reconstruction, the United States government was willing to give the respectable sum of $200 to $500 to the Northern branch of the Methodist Church to erect buildings in the South if the buildings were used as schools for "freedmen" during the week.[13] As to higher education for the first generation of ex-slaves, only spotty provision was being made. This was a source of great concern for Kelley.

When compared with most men, North and South, David Kelley held beliefs that were advanced on the subject of race. He did not accept the validity of racial equality, but neither did most Americans. It was this lack of national acceptance of the concept of racial equality that caused the United States government to abandon the attempt to make the Fourteenth and Fifteenth Amendments realities instead of words on paper. Kelley was consistent and vocal in his belief that it was the duty of Christians to aid the weak and to allow black people to become all they could be, albeit, while they remained in a position inferior to whites. In espousing this position, Kelley was echoing the ideas of his former commander, Nathan Bedford Forrest. While most of the public does not know, and while many historians are unwilling to admit it, Forrest evolved in his racial views so that he, too, was in advance of most people nationwide.[14]

In 1877, Kelley gave the commencement address at Tennessee Central College, an institution founded in 1865 by the Northern branch of the Methodist Church. In his address, Kelley referred to the students and faculty of this black college as "brethren, friends, and fellow citizens." He claimed "the feeling of personal regard and the relationship embraced in these names."[15] Tennessee Central College included a medical department, which survives today as Meharry Medical College.

Four years later, in 1881, Dr. Atticus Haygood, president of Emory University, published *Our Brother in Black*, in which he advocated college education for Negroes. By education of qualified students, Haygood argued, the economy of the entire South would be improved. The book aroused criticism in the church, and Kelley came to Haygood's defense, both from the pulpit and in writing. Kelley strongly defended the concept that the interest of both races was one and the same, and nowhere was this more important an issue than in the South.[16]

This outspoken advocacy of decent and fair treatment for African Americans did not go unnoticed in the black community. On April 4, 1883, the president of Fisk University, another church-sponsored school for freedmen, noted, "We have been cheered on our way over and over by the good works of such Southern men as Dr. Kelley."[17] W.E.B. Dubois was a student at Fisk at the time Kelley was publicly supporting the school and encouraging its students. Dubois was at Fisk because the colleges in his native Massachusetts were segregated and would not admit him.

It is a common attitude among those less well informed to consider the South the source of the nation's racial problem and to look at ex-Confederates as the origin of that problem. Such an attitude is not only not well informed, it is deliberately ignorant. The belief in Anglo-Saxon superiority has never been confined to the South nor did it originate there. Many ex-Confederates, such as Forrest, Kelley and George Washington Cable, were among those who, in the nineteenth century, advocated fair treatment for all men. A widespread belief in racial equality did not arise until the latter decades of the twentieth century, so Kelley's beliefs and actions place him in the advance guard on the issue of race for his day.

CONTROVERSY AT VANDERBILT

In 1875, Alexander Winchell was invited by Bishop McTyeire to become a part-time lecturer at Vanderbilt, offering twelve lectures during the spring semester. Winchell was a nationally known figure in the areas of geology and zoology; as such, he was on the fringes of the most rancorous of public debates, the scrutiny of the work of Charles Darwin. The publication of *On the Evolution of Species* in 1859 had begun the controversy, and the 1871 release of *The Descent of Man* had intensified it. It was in this second book that Darwin proposed that men and apes had a common ancestor, a view that challenged the popular religious view that humans were a "special creation" of God. Winchell did not concern himself with the origin of human beings, but he did write and lecture about the fossil record, pointing out that the world was of very ancient origin. The very fact that Winchell was a geologist made him suspect in the eyes of the more conservative leaders of the Methodist Episcopal Church, South. Although Winchell accepted numerous invitations to speak to church groups, usually meeting a positive response to his remarks, Dr. Thomas O. Summers, dean of religion at Vanderbilt, was hostile to him.

During the opening months of 1878, while away from Vanderbilt, Winchell published a pamphlet on "pre-Adamites," humans who existed before Adam. Winchell pointed out that the book of Genesis implies the existence of people in addition to Adam and Eve and their children; Cain married someone. This concept put Winchell at odds with the theories of Darwin, but it also made Winchell controversial. He conjectured that the pre-Adamites had been created first, that they came from Africa and that they were black.

By the end of the 1877–78 academic year, Winchell was under attack by several Methodist ministers. McTyeire had a conversation with Winchell and asked him to stay in Nashville beyond the end of his contract for the year in order to deliver a lecture as part of the commencement activities for the year. The suggested topic was evolution.[18] The speech was reported in the *Christian Advocate*, edited by Dean Summers:

> *On Monday, Founder's Day, the Board of Trust held two meetings—adjourning at 10 o'clock to hear a lecture from Dr. Winchell on "Man in the Light of Geology." It was one of the most beautiful lectures we have ever heard. It made us almost sorry we could not accept the nebular theory and evolution, its corollary; but nothing is clearer to our mind than that "special creation" is taught in Scripture—and we must abide by that.*[19]

This speech was actually delivered in the McKendree Methodist Church where Kelley was the pastor. As soon as the lecture was finished, the Board of Trust reassembled and voted to abolish the lectureship held by Winchell. David Kelley was the only member of the board to oppose this motion.

Although John J. Tigert, MyTyeire's biographer, argues that McTyeire thought that Winchell should have the freedom to express his views, the situation looks very much as if the bishop laid a trap for the professor.

Alexander Winchell, whose controversial views found a supporter in Kelley. *Courtesy Wisconsin Historical Society.*

Only forty-five minutes before the lecture was delivered, McTyeire had told Winchell that his continued presence was an embarrassment to the university and asked the professor to resign. Certainly, Winchell felt betrayed by McTyeire and said so in a lengthy letter to the *Daily American*.[20] By contrast, Kelley never in his career sought to silence those who upheld Darwin's theory, but neither did he argue for evolutionary views. Kelley appears to have thought that the matter of how God created the universe was unresolved and that the discussion should continue, with the caveat that creation was a divinely guided process. As a churchman, he had no fear of science, arguing, "All that is human in the standards of the church must be open to investigation and to improvement."[21]

For Kelley, truth was truth, no matter what discipline revealed it. If science revealed truth, then religion should accept it since all truth ultimately came from God. This open-minded attitude concerning free inquiry and academic freedom marks Kelley as the sort of person who would fit well into a university setting in the twenty-first century but as the sort who was rare in the nineteenth. At the time, however, Kelley was clearly a minority at Vanderbilt University. Across the nation, academic leaders condemned the treatment of Winchell, and the reputation of Vanderbilt sank. It would be many years before the university had a chance to redeem its reputation as a place where free inquiry was valued. The official organs of the Methodist Church praised the board, but this "in-house" praise did not help the standing of Vanderbilt.

The stand taken by Kelley did not damage his standing in the church despite the unpopularity of any idea associated with evolution. Kelley's stand in support of free and open debate was rejected, but his personal popularity as a preacher and his war record of audacious leadership protected his place in the church. In 1879, he received an appointment that allowed him to pursue a lifelong passion; Kelley became an official of the Methodist Board of Missions. In carrying out his duties, Kelley was a frequent contributor to church publications, and he traveled widely, speaking to numerous congregations and conferences in support of the mission objectives of the Methodist Episcopal Church, South. He would remain in this capacity until 1888.

By this time, David and his second wife, Mary Owen Campbell Kelley, had established a family of their own. From his first marriage David had three children living: Daisy (born 1858), John Harris (born 1860) and Elizabeth (born 1862). With Mary Owen, David became the father of Margaret Lavinia (born 1869), William Bowen (born 1871), David Jr. (born 1873) and Owen Campbell (born 1874). In 1877, Daisy married Walter Russell Lambuth, who would rise to the office of bishop in the Methodist Church.

THE PREACHER AND THE ACTRESS

On October 3, 1887, the Vendome Theater opened its doors at 615 Church Street in Nashville. This Moorish-style building was built as an opera house

Kelley disagreed with Warren Aiken Candler's views on proper social behavior. *Courtesy of Emory University.*

with two balconies and sixteen boxes. It could seat a total of 1,600 patrons. The opening of this lavish building was a major social event for Nashville, especially since a celebrity had been booked to play the leading female role in *Il Trovatore*. This celebrity was Emma Abbott.[22]

Emma Abbott was born in Chicago in 1850 and began performing as a child in 1859 because her family needed the money. In 1866, Abbott became a friend of Clara Kellogg, a leading singer of the day, and with the help of her new friend, Emma Abbott received formal training in New York and, later, in Europe. In 1876, she married Eugene Wetherall, and the two formed an opera company known as the Abbott English Opera Company. The company always sang in English, much to the displeasure of music critics but to the delight of large audiences.[23]

One block down Church Street, at number 523, stood (and stands) McKendree Methodist Church. In 1887, McKendree was the leading Methodist church in Nashville and was one of the trend-setting congregations of that denomination in the South. The church had a new pastor, the Reverend Doctor W.A. Candler. Mr. Candler was a leading spokesman in the movement opposing "worldly amusements." This phrase covered all sorts of activities, including reading novels, playing cards, round (as opposed to "square") dancing, organized sports and theater attendance. While none of these activities was overtly condemned in the scriptures, the Methodist Episcopal Church, South, objected to them because "they could not be used in the name of the Lord Jesus," to cite a phrase commonly found in pamphlets and sermons on the topic. This lack of firm religious use was thought to be a slippery slope that would lead to immorality. Candler was concerned that Methodist schools for young ladies had classes in elocution, as these classes often required the students to recite passages from classic plays. Candler felt that learning these passages might lead to the desire to attend a performance of the entire play.

Thus, when the Vendome opened just a block down the street and when its nightly packed house included parishioners of McKendree Methodist, Candler felt it was time for an authoritative pronouncement from the pulpit. That pronouncement was delivered as the morning sermon on October 9. Dr. Candler took his text from Acts 19:29 and proceeded to quote writers from the days of ancient Greece down to his contemporaries, all of whom condemned the immoral nature of plays and attendance at the theater. Candler went on to say, "You say that preaching this way will divide the church. If it divides McKendree Church I will thank God that we will have the sound half on our side. I don't believe in putting up good and rotten apples together. It will spoil the whole lot. We can spare two or three hundred and still have a fair church here."[24]

Emma Abbott had walked down from the Maxwell House Hotel at the corner of Fourth and Church Streets and was sitting, unrecognized, in a rear pew. At the conclusion of the sermon, she stood up and rebuked the pastor: "I cannot refrain from expressing my indignation that a minister ordained to preach Christ should so far forget his mission, and so far depart from the truth, as to make the assertions to which I have listened regarding the profession

Kelley defended the actress Emma Abbott against attacks by his fellow ministers. *Courtesy of the Peoria, Illinois Public Library.*

of which I am, I trust, an honored member. There are among us men and women who have sinned, as there are men in every calling who have disgraced their professions."

She went on to list several actors and actresses who were well known for their support of the church and reminded the congregation that all knew of ministers who had sinned publicly. There was a burst of applause from the pews, and then the final hymn was announced, "All Hail the Power of Jesus' Name." The soaring voice of the diva hushed the audience so that she sang most of the hymn as a solo and was greeted at the end by another burst of applause.[25]

Abbott returned to the Maxwell House, where news of her actions had preceded her. Not only did applause sweep the dining room but a collection was taken by some of the diners and Emma was presented a very large bouquet. On Monday morning, the event was front-page news in Nashville and as far away as Chicago and New York.[26]

On October 12, an unsigned letter appeared in the *Daily American* in which the author, described by the editor of the paper as "an eminent Divine," challenged Candler's remarks as "extreme and uninformed." The letter concluded:

> *There are few educated, refined Christian people who would not have chosen the attitude of Miss Abbott on that Sunday to the preacher's—her discriminating applause of the noble in the profession to his uncharitable, universal denunciations. The defense of her spotless name, which at the close of a week of honest work, she found so rudely assailed, not by a ruffian, but by a preacher.*[27]

By this time Candler was furious, and the Board of McKendree Church had met to issue a resolution of support of his position. Bishop McTyeire had been at the meeting when the resolution had been adopted and had spoken strongly in support of Candler's stand. Candler then approached the editor of the *Daily American* only to have his request refused. A few days later, Kelley acknowledged that he was the author, sending personal notes to Candler and to McTyeire as well as publishing another letter in the paper accepting authorship. This raised the level of controversy to new heights, and the matter continued to be fought over in the church press long after the daily papers had lost interest in the matter. Candler defined his position in the pages of the *Christian Advocate*, and virtually every Methodist paper in the South sided with him. Kelley found he had attacked a position too strong for him to carry and was left with only the option of keeping his head down until his opponents had fired off all their ammunition. For a time it looked as if Kelley would lose his job at the mission board, but in December, a rather meek note in the *Christian Advocate* stated that Kelley had only intended to help Candler be less harsh.[28]

Kelley was twenty years older than Candler and had fought through a war that Candler had experienced only as a child. It seems that his life experiences and his greater experience in the ministry led Kelley to be more gentle in his treatment of those who committed peccadilloes than was the habit of the more conservative Candler. It also seems that Kelley had a warm place in his heart for the McKendree congregation, and to him Candler's talk of casually allowing two or three hundred members to leave over an issue such as attending an opera was destructive to the church. However, on this occasion Kelley found himself well in advance of public opinion. The Methodist Church actually tightened its rules dealing with entertainment, and the issue did not become moot until changing social customs vindicated Kelley's views more than six decades later. Fortunately, Kelley remembered from his days as a soldier how to make a strategic retreat, and he survived to be a voice calling for change in Methodist circles.

THE PREACHER ON TRIAL

In the decade of the 1840s, the Prohibition movement began to gain strength in the United States. Distilling had a long history in the nation and had been practiced in most rural areas as a solution to the problem of getting crops to market. Converting corn to whiskey or turning fruit into brandy reduced the bulk and weight of the commodities as well as making them into an imperishable item. In addition, alcohol was widely used for medicinal purposes, either mixed with herbal concoctions or used diluted with water. As better medicine became available, and as the steam engine began to provide faster transportation via steamboats and railroads, these rationales for producing alcoholic beverages began to disappear.

During the War Between the States, many prominent Confederates were known to be total abstainers from liquor. Among these were Robert E. Lee, "Stonewall" Jackson, J.E.B. Stuart and Nathan Bedford Forrest. Their example reinforced the moral structures of many churches, including the Methodist Episcopal Church, South, which forbade its members to drink liquor.

As the Prohibition movement progressed beyond the state of personal decision to involve a public crusade against liquor, led by the Woman's

Christian Temperance Union (WCTU) and fiery advocates such as Carrie Nation, the movement turned toward politics as a means of achieving the goal of a "dry" nation. This left many churches in a dilemma. Like many others, the Methodist Church in the South had a strong tradition of being silent on political issues. This tradition was one of the factors that had led to the sectional division of the church in the 1840s when the Northern branch began to speak against slavery while the Southern branch viewed the issue as a political and not a moral question. This meant the Methodist Church, along with others, opposed liquor on moral grounds but also opposed involvement with a Prohibitionist political party. The church said it was "a prohibition church and not a party church," as a common phrase put the proposition.

David C. Kelley questioned the position of the church. He felt that refusing to pursue a political solution to a moral question was bad strategy. Kelley was part of a military and militant tradition that held that the enemy should be hit with everything available.

In 1890, the leaders of the Tennessee Prohibition Party asked Kelley to be their candidate for governor. As Kelley considered what to do, his heart told him one thing, but his church told him something different. On June 25, just after being asked to run for governor, Kelley wrote his bishop, Dr. J.C. Keener, asking for guidance. As pastor of the church at Gallatin, Tennessee, Kelley knew he would not have time to conduct an effective campaign and continue to hold services at the church. He planned to get a substitute to preach and to give up his salary while a candidate, but he sought approval for his actions. Kelley told Bishop Keener that he would refuse the party's nomination if the bishop objected to his making the race. In July, Keener replied that Kelley could decide for himself which was the better response to God's calling, pursuing the candidacy or functioning as pastor at Gallatin.[29] On July 20, Presiding Elder B.F. Haynes announced that a retired minister, the Reverend W.G. Davis, would assume the pulpit duties at Gallatin, effective on August 1.[30]

At this point, Kelley had made a mistake. Obviously, Presiding Elder Haynes should have involved Bishop Keener in the decision to name an interim at Gallatin. Also, Kelley had the option of asking his bishop to give him a "location," an assignment to non-pastoral duties. Neither of these steps was taken, opening Kelley to attack by those who disapproved of his tactics in assisting the cause of Prohibition and by those who simply did not like Kelley. There were some of both of these in Tennessee Methodist circles.

In October 1890, the Tennessee Annual Conference of the church met in Pulaski. When Kelley arrived at the meeting, he was told by several friends that newly installed Bishop R.K. Hargrove intended to try Kelley on a charge of deserting his post at Gallatin. However, Methodist canon law required that Kelley receive prior notice of such charges, and none had been presented to him. At the conference session of October 11, the annual report from the Gallatin church was called for. Presiding Elder Haynes called on Kelley to give the report. This was immediately met by an objection by Reverend G.W. Winn, who stated that Kelley had "left his work" and that this was reason for "arresting Kelley's character"—that is, Winn was preferring charges and calling for Kelley to be put on trial.[31]

Objections and counter-objections flew across the assembly, but these were ended for a moment when Bishop Hargrove ruled that as chair of the conference he had the authority to appoint a Committee of Investigation to determine if Kelley should be tried on the charges stated. Members appointed to the committee were T.B. Fisher, A.T. Goodloe and J.A. Orman. Fisher had served as a private under Kelley on the second day of the Battle of Nashville. He and Goodloe had already spoken from the floor expressing views opposing the actions Kelley had taken. The conference was not surprised that this Committee of Investigation quickly returned a report calling for Kelley to be tried on the charge that he had deserted his pulpit. This was a very serious charge since, if sustained, it carried the possible penalty of being defrocked. A motion was made by a Kelley supporter that the conference not concur with the report of the committee. This motion of non-concurrence carried by a vote of 116 to 25. Clearly, his fellow ministers largely stood by Kelley. Following this show of support, a motion was made to "pass the character" of David Kelley, but Bishop Hargrove ruled the motion "out of order." A new Committee of Investigation was appointed, made up of men who had just voted against Kelley. These men were J.D. Barbee, T.K. Kerley and L.C. Bryant. The bishop further ruled that the conference would not vote on their report. Of course, the report called for a trial, and Barbee and Kerley were named prosecutors. The jury that would hear the evidence was chosen from among the 25 who had voted against Kelley on the first attempt to bring him to trial.[32]

Monday, October 14, was the date for the trial. Bishop Hargrove ruled against all the motions offered in favor of Kelley's defense, and the outcome of the proceedings was a predictable verdict of "guilty." The penalty, however, was a moderate one: six months suspension from ministerial duties.[33] This would not be the end of the matter.

The Methodist church in Pulaski where Kelley stood trial.

In many ways, the trial was the result of the style in which Kelley pursued his calling as minister. The vote of non-concurrence on the report of the first Committee of Investigation shows that Kelley was very popular among his fellow ministers. In their ranks, Kelley was seen as a champion for the rights of the individual against the unbridled authority of the hierarchy; he was the voice of those who had the hard, sometimes dull, always demanding business of carrying on the ministry of the church at the local level. For all his postwar career, however, Kelley was seen by the hierarchy as a rebel. On evolution, on questions of personal behavior and on social issues Kelley was

Kelley's chapel, constructed under the supervision of Kelley while he was presiding elder of the Nashville District.

avant garde. He was often in public opposition to the views and practices of the church leadership. In a letter to the *Christian Advocate*, Chancellor Landon Garland of Vanderbilt branded Kelley a maverick and stated that Kelley often acted without mature consideration, although no one could question his motives. Also, Kelley traveled widely and his appealing personality garnered him supporters wherever he went. Some of these trips lasted as much as six weeks and took him all over the South. If Kelley was indeed a maverick, he was a dangerous one.[34] The response of Kelley and his supporters to the decision of the jury was to draw up an appeal to the College of Bishops. This appeal included an accusation that Bishop Hargrove had knowingly loaded the Committee of Investigation and the trial body with men known to oppose Kelley. Hargrove was also accused of acting in an autocratic fashion and of ignoring the rights guaranteed ministers by Methodist canon law.

In the midst of the furor of the discussion surrounding the trial and appeal, the heart and mind of David Kelley were tragically elsewhere. On November 17, 1890, the Nashville Ministerial Association noted in its minutes its regret at the death of Mrs. Mary Campbell Kelley. Just before her last breath, Mary Kelley was reported to have said to her husband, "Thank God He let me die when you were at home. The hardest thing I have to do is to forgive your enemies who have been so unjust."[35] This personal tragedy also distracted Kelley from the results of the election, which was won by the Democratic candidate, John P. Buchanan. The winning candidate had also received strong support from the Farmers and Labor Party, a splinter of the growing Populist movement. Even so, Kelley received the largest number of votes ever tallied by a Prohibition candidate in Tennessee.

The suspension period ended for Kelley in 1891, and he was posted to the Springfield, Tennessee church. During his tenure there, Kelley's appeal came before the College of Bishops at their meeting in Wilmington, North Carolina, in May 1891. The college sustained the procedural rulings Bishop Hargrove had made, but on the key issue of who should have appointed the trial committee, the college ruled that the conference had that right, thus vindicating Kelley.[36] With this victory, Kelley became even more popular. He was sent on speaking tours by Prohibition supporters and was invited to be the guest speaker at numerous Methodist functions. He returned to Nashville in 1893 and 1894 as pastor of the Elm Street Church. When Thomas Fisher, one of the men who had opposed Kelley at his Pulaski trial, was named to succeed Kelley at Elm Street, a great many church members withheld their financial support, and Fisher's salary was reduced by $1,200, a very large reduction.[37] In 1894, the General Conference of the Methodist Church, South, met and Kelley carried the day. Not only was the action of Bishop Hargrove reversed but the canon law was revised to make clear that conferences, not bishops, had the right to appoint committees to try ministers facing charges.[38]

God's warrior could say, in the words of the motto of the Confederate States of America, *Deo Vindice*: "God Vindicates My Cause."

Chapter 5

Old Battlefields Revisited

FORREST VETERANS ASSOCIATION

David C. Kelley was a prolific writer. He produced a flood of articles for church publications, he wrote books on religious topics and his sermons frequently found their way into print. Kelley did not write an account of his personal military career, nor has a collection of private papers about the war been preserved. This does not mean Kelley had no interest in revisiting his military career—he did. But Kelley always focused his wartime reminiscences on others, not on himself.

Following the resolution of the controversy surrounding his run for governor, Kelley became active in the United Confederate Veterans. By the standards of his day, Kelley had reached old age, and his desire to have greater association with other veterans was part of the process of reviewing the accomplishments of his life. The UCV was organized in 1889 and brought together numerous smaller, local groups that had been formed by veterans. Kelley's war record, his association with Bedford Forrest and his intelligence soon made him a leading figure in the UCV.

When Confederate veterans from across the South convened in Atlanta in 1896, Kelley was present and was asked to serve as chairman of the Committee on Resolutions.[1] This experience with the leadership of the UCV opened Kelley's eyes to the potential power the group could exert. The next year, as part of the plans for the centennial celebration of statehood for Tennessee, Kelley wrote a column for the *Confederate Veteran* calling for a "Forrest Day Rally" to be held as part of the celebration. As the only surviving officer of Forrest's original command, commonly called "Forrest's Old Regiment," Kelley wrote:

> *In view of the fact that Forrest is rapidly becoming recognized as the greatest of Tennessee soldiers, it is eminently proper that his old soldiers should meet in a grand rally one day during the Tennessee Centennial. As the oldest survivor of his first military family, I wrote to suggest that we have a Forrest Day, that all comrades who at any time served with him be present, first in military parade and then in historic celebration.*

As a result of the planning for the rally, a Forrest Veterans Association was organized, and Kelley was elected one of its officers. The organizational meeting of this association was held at the Fogg School in downtown Nashville, a building still standing in 2010 and known as Hume-Fogg High School. The constitution of the organization declared that "the objects of the association are to bring together annually the soldiers who may at any time have served under the command of Lieutenant General Forest for good fellowship, the collection of accurate historical data, and the creation of a memorial worthy of our great commander."

H.B. Lyon was chosen head of the new group, with Kelley and R.B. McCullough as lieutenant commanders. George L. Cowan was the adjutant or secretary/treasurer.[2] Cowan had married Hattie McGavock, daughter of John and Carrie McGavock of Carton Plantation at Franklin, Tennessee. Forrest's Escort Company and Staff had formed a veterans' association as early as 1877. Kelley was a member of that group by virtue of having been adjutant of Forrest's original regiment.[3]

Also in 1897, Kelley traveled to the battlefield of Fort Donelson to take part in dedicating the Fort Donelson Memorial Chapel. This was actually the Methodist church in the town of Dover. The original building had been destroyed in the early days of the war, and the site of the church became the camp of the 83rd Illinois. When the church was destroyed, a U.S. soldier took the pulpit Bible and sent it to his family in Illinois. The church building Kelley was helping dedicate had been built with donations from former soldiers from both the North and the South. Above the main entrance was a large stained-glass window showing a Union and a Confederate soldier shaking hands. In his dedicatory speech, Kelley said some things that were very revealing about his changing attitude toward religion, society, race and politics. Kelley renounced the view held by the Methodist Episcopal Church in the antebellum period that had made moral and political issues off limits for discussion in the church. Kelley argued that "religion is not a transportation society designed to get people to heaven but it is a means to make our daily lives the best possible and the world we live in a heaven." Christians could not ignore a known wrong, as the church had done with slavery, for to do so was to court danger and disaster. "Delay in confronting wrong because of difficulty is no excuse," he added. Just as the church could have prevented the Civil War had it addressed the issue of slavery, so the church could prevent much wrong by addressing the current issue of Prohibition.

Kelley closed his remarks by recounting his experiences during the battle at Fort Donelson. Forrest left the cavalry under the command of Major David Kelley and went to observe the Confederate artillery as it battled the gunboats. Shortly after, Forrest returned to report that the 32-pounders were useless, their shots "roll off the boats like water off a duck's back." Another visit to the artillery brought the report that the 120-pounder had "kicked off the carriage leaving only a single 64 pounder." Forrest then said, "Are you praying? Pray, Major, only God Almighty can save us. WE have no power to look to but God and one gun."[4]

The response of men proud to say "I rode with Forrest" was overwhelming. Meetings of the Forrest Veterans Association became regular features of conventions of the UCV, plus the association often met on its own. Perhaps the most significant meeting of the association took place in 1900. Kelley was commander of the Forrest Veterans Association, assisted by Charles Anderson, once acting assistant adjutant under Forrest. These two arranged for a meeting of the old veterans at Brice's Cross Roads, the site of the most spectacular of all Forrest's victories. As the men met on their field of glory, Kelley emphasized to them that no suitable monument marked the burial place of their great leader. The veterans responded to the challenge, and a committee was named, with Kelley as chair, to raise money to bring to completion the plan of erecting a suitable monument, a project that had been underway since 1891. Serving on the committee with Kelley were Charles Anderson, W.A. Collier of Memphis and George L. Cowan, former first lieutenant in Forrest's Escort.[5]

THE FORREST MONUMENT

Interest in the monument project was further stimulated by the appearance of a biography of Forrest. The eminent surgeon and ex-Confederate cavalryman John Allan Wyeth brought out *Life of General Nathan Bedford*

Forrest in 1899. By 1900, the book was selling widely across the entire nation. The book is still in print more than a century later, now published as *That Devil Forrest*. Kelley wrote a review of Wyeth's work in the *Methodist Review*, interspersing personal remarks about his association with Forrest alongside comments about Wyeth's words. Kelley had provided Wyeth with material about Forrest and his campaigns. It was Kelley who had first given the famous description of Forrest in combat: "His face flushed until he bore a striking resemblance to a painted Indian warrior, and his eyes, usually so mild in their expression, flashed with the intense glare of the panther about to spring on its prey. In fact, he looked as little like the Forrest of our mess table as the storm of December resembles the quiet of June."[6]

Although the poor economy of the South had made the project a lengthy one, the cause of memorializing Forrest struck an emotional chord, and by 1901, enough money had been raised so that the cornerstone for the monument was laid and dedicated. The UCV convention was held in Memphis that year. The members of the Forrest Veterans Association were out in force, and Kelley saw to it that the cornerstone dedication was the focal point of the meeting.[7]

The capstone of Kelley's activities with the veterans came in 1905. Not only did he lead the Forrest Veterans Association in the parade that was part of the UCV meeting in Louisville, but he also returned to Memphis for the unveiling of the Forrest statue. Judge J.P. Young, a former trooper under Forrest, served as master of ceremonies. General George W. Gordon gave the dedicatory address, but the most unusual feature of the day was the speech given by Colonel C.A. Stanton, 3rd Iowa Cavalry, U.S.A. Stanton had led his men against Forrest for two years and had come to admire the Confederate general greatly. Stanton noted: "Impartial history has given General Forrest high rank as one of the greatest cavalry leaders of modern times. No American, North or South, now seeks to lessen the measure of his fame, and no one can speak of him without remembrance of the men who served with him and whose soldierly qualities made it possible for him to win his wonderful victories."

After all the introductions of UDC chapters that had worked so tirelessly to make the statue a reality, Kelley had the last word. He gave the benediction. Kelley said:

> *Gen. N.B. Forrest, whose statue and monument we here unveil, did not need this tribute at our hands; it was needed that we might in some way prove ourselves worthy to have been his comrades and co-patriots.*

Gen. Joseph E. Johnston has already said Forrest was the greatest soldier the war produced. Gen. Dabney Maury has said Forrest, the greatest soldier of the generation.

Gen. W.T. Sherman, the great Federal leader, declared Forrest to be the greatest military genius the war produced.

Yet we, his old comrades and fellow-citizens, needed in self-vindication to mold into imperishable form this, our form of expression. It was my fortune to have been his second in command in his first regiment, to have been with him in his first battle; to have surrendered with him when the war ended. The further privilege was mine to have been his messmate during the first year of the war; to have seen him bow reverently when divine blessing was invoked at the mess table and at daily evening prayer; to witness his acts of tenderest sympathy for suffering women and wounded comrades; his marvelous charm for little children.

When, by the too great kindness of our surviving comrades, I was elected to the command of the veteran cavalry corps which bears his name today, when acknowledging the honor, the pledge was made that our work should be first to give to our generation a true history of the man the world knows him today. Second, to build a monument to his name. At the foot of this majestic memorial I, today offer the thanks of his comrades for what you have done, and to add my resignation.

For as much as God, our Father, has put it into the hearts of our fellow-citizens and comrades to erect this monument in memory of Gen. Nathan Bedford Forrest, we here dedicate it to the promotion of patriotism, chivalry and devotion to country as God gave him to see these duties. We reverently return our thanks to Almighty God for His gift to us of this man, and this inspiration to virtue of the citizens who, in the erection of the monument, prove themselves not unworthy of God's gift to the an. God the Father, God the Son and God the Holy Ghost keep us in memory of past heroism and future reverent obedience. Amen! [8]

Age was taking its toll on David Kelley. He contributed pieces to the *Confederate Veteran* dealing with mistakes made at the Battle of Shiloh, and he wrote a sketch of the life of General Alexander Peter Stewart. In 1906, he gave up his position as commander of the Forrest Veterans Association, and he stopped traveling long distances to attend conventions of the UCV, although he did attend smaller events that were held closer to his home. In 1906 and 1908, he was present at the meetings of the Escort and Staff Association and served as chaplain of these gatherings.[9]

THE DEVIL'S PARSON

In 1908, Kelley submitted an article to the *Confederate Veteran* in which one gets a glimpse of his war experiences but that reveals even more about a topic to which very little attention has been paid—the religious nature of Nathan Bedford Forrest. Northern opponents sometimes called Forrest "that devil," but Kelley had been "the devil's parson." In the article, Kelley says:

> *The writer was associated with General Forrest from a very early period in the war, first in the Forrest Cavalry Regiment, our regimental headquarters being one. We had one table and, for a time, one tent; family prayers in the evening and grace at meals. The son (William, usually called "Willie") was a member with his mother (Mary Ann Montgomery Forrest) of the First Cumberland Presbyterian Church in Memphis. By his father's consent he became my deacon and elder, performing both functions. Later, when General Forrest was commanding a division or corps, the son was still charged with conveying orders for religious services to be held at headquarters. With the genteel and devout bearing of his mother, commingled with the activities of his father, he conveyed the orders for headquarters services or cared for the preacher's comfort, so we came to know and love each other well.*
>
> *Since the close of the war I was able to decipher one problem or connect it, especially with William. General Forrest made a visit to General Polk's headquarters, about two days' ride distant, and returned with two soldier youths who possessed the highest blood of our South land—one the son of Bishop Otey, of the Episcopal Church; the other a son of General Donelson, of Tennessee. For more than two years they had been under the care of Bishop-General Polk. Forrest never told us that it was for companions to Willie in that military life, to meet the anxiety and Christian culture of the mother when her health would no longer allow her to keep near headquarters, watching over this boy. The General had for once forgotten battle and hardship that she might feel comfort in the knowledge that the companionship of the only son was with charming youths of the highest birth and truest courage. This is written that the fame of the father in battle may not obscure the higher and nobler characteristics of desire for Christian training and association for the son. Yet Willie was brave as pure. Many a night the writer shared his blanket.*[10]

On another occasion, Kelley recalled of Forrest:

> *He had absolute confidence in the piety of his mother and wife, and was himself a thorough believer in Christianity, was as fully persuaded of the efficacy of prayer in times of danger or in battle as Napoleon was a believer in fate. Throughout the war he always gave me the fullest opportunities for preaching in camp, courteously entertaining at his mess-table all preachers whom I might choose to invite. He was always present at such services when it was practicable. While we were messmates there was always family prayer in his tent at night conducted by the chaplain and myself.*
>
> *On one of our expeditions a chaplain of the Federal army was overtaken and captured. When he learned that he was to be taken to Forrest's headquarters, every feature showed the deepest anxiety and depression. As he approached, General Forrest bade him be seated while he attended to other matters. A little later supper was announced, and the chaplain was requested to share our meal with us. When all were seated, Forrest turned to him reverentially and said: "Parson, will you please ask the blessing?" The minister could not conceal his surprise, which was evident from the manner in which he looked at Forrest before being assured that he was in earnest. He gave expression to the gratitude he felt at being thus considerately treated. He had evidently been expecting to be killed by this fierce fighter. The next morning Forrest gave him an escort through our lines, telling him that he had no war to make on non-combatants, and humorously remarked to him as he bade him good-bye, "Parson, I would keep you here to preach for me if you were not needed so much more by the sinners on the other side."*[11]

One of the favorite groups of associates enjoyed by Kelley was the men who had served as Forrest's personal escort. These men had been recruited for the task of being the bodyguards of the general and had never been connected with a regiment, serving throughout the war as an independent company. In 1877, just weeks before his death, Forrest had met with many of these men, and they, along with surviving members of Forrest's staff, had formed a veterans' association. Kelley attended many of their annual reunions and was often a featured speaker. By 1909, so few of these men were left alive that they decided to hold their last reunion in the town of Shelbyville, Tennessee, the place where they had been organized in 1862. Kelley missed the meeting; his health had become too fragile for him to make the fifty-five-mile trip from Nashville to Shelbyville, despite the two towns being connected by a railroad.

The monument at Confederate Circle, Mount Olivet Cemetery, Nashville, overlooks David Kelley's final resting place.

The end came peaceably for David C. Kelley. As the summer came on and the weather became hot and oppressive, he had less and less energy. On May 19, 1909, at the home of his daughter, Mrs. W.R. Lambuth, located at 2501 West End Avenue, the old soldier answered his last roll call. At the end, he said to the assembled members of his family, "My work is done."[12]

The *Confederate Veteran* noted:

> *Reverend D.C. Kelley, D.D., was born in Leesville, Wilson County, Tennessee, in 1823, and died in Nashville in 1909. He was sent as a missionary to Chine by the Methodist Episcopal Church, South, and for years did very noble work in propagating Christianity in that far-off land. On his return to America he organized a company of cavalry which was called Kelley's Troop and which served under General N.B. Forrest, and was with that gallant commander during the war. D.C. Kelley so distinguished himself for coolness in action and bravery in the face of danger that he was rapidly promoted, being made major of battalion. He was elected Lt Col of Forrest's Regiment the day before the battle of Shiloh, and took the duty of Colonel in the battle of Murfreesboro. He was on Forrest's staff as chaplain and aid. Afterward, he commanded a regiment, then a brigade till the end of the war, winning a brilliant reputation as "Forrest's Fighting Preacher." At the end of the war he was made pastor of several of the largest Methodist churches in Tennessee. Here his influence for good was widely felt, as in his upright life and true Christianity he was an example of what a noble man should be.*[13]

David Campbell Kelley was, indeed, an example of what a noble man should be. He was dedicated to his calling as a man of God and as a man of war. He fought bravely for the Confederate cause and in the cause of the church militant. He accepted the decisions of history without flinching and moved on to confront the next challenge. Throughout his long and active life, he was a man whose place was at the front of the line, a man who had the ability and the willingness to lead. He was a fighting preacher of the first order.

Notes

Chapter 1

1. DescendentsofDavidKelley.com.
2. DescendentsofBlackDavidCampbell.com; Pilcher, "Sketch of Captain David Campbell," pp154ff.
3. "West Wilson County Neighbors," *Mt. Juliet—West Wilson County Historical Society*, n.d., 20–21. The community where David Campbell Kelley was born is now called "Leeville," a name it received following the War Between the States in honor of Robert E. Lee. Originally, the community was called "Stringtown," since it was "strung out along the road," or it was called "Kelley's Church."
4. TNGenWeb, "Wilson County—Leeville."
5. David C. Kelley to John and Margaret Kelley, August 14, 1848. Box 24, Campbell Papers.
6. David Campbell to John and Margaret Kelley, August 16, 1848. Box 24, Campbell Papers.
7. David C. Kelley to Mary Kelley, August 18, 1848. Box 24, Campbell Papers. The inn at Beersheba Springs still stands and is a conference center for the United Methodist Church.
8. David C. Kelley to Margaret Kelley, September 4, 1848. Box 24, Campbell Papers.
9. David C. Kelley to unknown, November 24, 1852. Box 26, Campbell Papers.
10. David C. Kelley to unknown, December 6, 1852. Box 26, Campbell Papers.

11. David C. Kelley to John and Margaret Kelley, December 17, 1852. Box 26, Campbell Papers.

12. David C. Kelley to Margaret Kelley, September 7, 1853. Box 27, Campbell Papers.

13. David C. Kelley to Margaret Kelle,. September 10, 1853. Box 27, Campbell Papers.

14. www.familytreemaker.genealogy.com.JamesTKelley. Inscription on Manerva Amanda Harris Kelley's tombstone. Cedar Grove Cemetery, Lebanon, Tennessee.

15. Kelley, "Memoirs of a Seventeen Year Old."

16. Ibid.

17. Mary Owen Campbell to William B. Campbell, April 10, 1854. Box 28, Campbell Papers. Mary Owen Campbell had received a letter from Margaret Lavinia Kelley with a description of the trip from Lebanon to New York City. Mary Owen sent her father a digest of the contents of that letter. Diary of Margaret Lavinia Kelley. Hereinafter cited as Margaret Kelley Diary.

18. William Campbell to David Campbell, January 5, 1855. Box 29, Campbell Papers; William Campbell to David Campbell, January 10, 1855. Box 29, Campbell Papers; William Campbell to Virginia Campbell, February 10, 1855. Box 29, Campbell Papers; William Campbell to David Campbell, May 12, 1855. Box 29, Campbell Papers. In all these letters, William Campbell is passing on a digest of news received in letters that no longer exist.

19. Manerva Amanda Harris Kelley to Mary Owen Campbell, May 17, 1855. Box 29, Campbell Papers.

20. Lizzie Maney Kelley, "Memoirs of a Seventeen Year Old."

21. David Campbell Kelley, Church Service Record.

CHAPTER 2

1. *Confederate Veteran* 19 (1911): 291.

2. Steenburn, *The Man Called Gurley*, 34.

3. Rice, *Hard Times*, 46.

4. Thomason, *Jeb Stuart*, 79.

5. Rice, *Hard Times*, 48. The unit to which Kelley was assigned had a varied history during the course of the war. It became a regiment-sized unit in 1862 and then was divided into two battalions, with the Huntsville contingent becoming Company K of Russell's Fourth Alabama Cavalry. The rest of the unit was known at various times as Balch's Battalion, McDonald's Battalion, 26th Tennessee Battalion, 3rd Tennessee Cavalry

Regiment or "Forrest's Old Regiment." When Kelley became major of the battalion, James M. Hambrick became captain of the company.

6. Otey and Kwok, "A Chinese Confederate Veteran," part 37, 1; Kwok, "Kate in a Heathen Land."

7. *Huntsville Democrat*, October 16, 1861.

8. Wyeth, *That Devil Forrest*, 24.

9. *Huntsville Democrat*, October 2, 1861.

10. Rice, *Hard Times*, 48.

11. Service record of David C. Kelley, Tennessee State Library and Archives. Hereinafter cited as Kelley service record. Cunningham served in the Confederate Quartermaster Department throughout the war, moving south as military necessity required. He ended the war in Augusta, Georgia.

12. Corder Manuscript.

13. Ibid.

14. Jordan and Pryor, *Campaigns of General Nathan Bedford Forrest*, fn, 46.

15. Naval History Home Page, USN ships, USS *Conestoga*; Slagle, *Ironclad Captain*, 145.

16. Jordan and Pryor, *Campaigns of General Nathan Bedford Forrest*, fn., 49.

17. Wyeth, *That Devil Forrest*, 27.

18. Wyeth, "Appearance and Characteristics of Forrest," 41.

19. Blanton, "Forrest's Old Regiment," 41.

20. *Official Records of the War of the Rebellion*, vol. 7, 65. Hereafter cited as *O.R.*; Jordan and Pryor, *Campaigns of General Nathan Bedford Forrest*, fn., 49.

21. Lindsley, *Military Annals of Tennessee*, vol. 2, 762; *O.R.* 7, 383.

22. *O.R.* 7, 383–84; Hurst, *Men of Fire*, 184–85.

23. Cooling, *Forts Henry and Donelson*, 154–55.

24. Blanton, "Forrest's Old Regiment," 41.

25. Wyeth, *That Devil Forrest*, 41.

26. Ibid., 558–59.

27. Hurst, *Men of Fire*, 234.

28. *O.R.* 7, 384–85; Hurst, *Men of Fire*, 235–36.

29. *O.R.* 7, 385; Hurst, *Men of Fire*, 247.

30. *O.R.* 7, 385; Hurst, *Men of Fire*, 254.

31. *O.R.* VII, 385; Hurst, *Men of Fire*, 258–59. In this charge on McAllister's Battery, Captain Charles May was killed. May had been a lieutenant in McDonald's company, raised near New Madrid, and had joined Forrest with that unit. May was then invited to help raise an additional company and became its captain. May emphasized drill and discipline in his unit, as did the other company commanders under Forrest. This attention to drill produced the ability to maneuver under fire and helped lay the foundation for the success of the regiment at Donelson. May's body

was sent to Nashville the day he was killed and was taken from there to Memphis, where he was buried in Elmwood Cemetery.

32. Jordan and Pryor, *Campaigns of General Nathan Bedford Forrest*, 84.
33. Cooling, *Forts Henry and Donelson*, 205–7; Hurst, *Men of Fire*, 323–24; *O.R.* 7, 386.
34. Jordan and Pryor, *Campaigns of General Nathan Bedford Forrest*, 101.
35. Ibid., 102–3; Durham, *Nashville*, 36–37.
36. Margaret Kelley Diary, February 25, 1862; Jordan and Pryor, *Campaigns of General Nathan Bedford Forrest*, 105.
37. Jordan and Pryor, *Campaigns of General Nathan Bedford Forrest*, 106; Wyeth, *That Devil Forrest*, 60; Hurst, *Nathan Bedford Forrest*, 87.
38. Familytreemaker.geneaology.com. Descendents of Dennis Kelley.
39. Jordan and Pryor, *Campaigns of General Nathan Bedford Forrest*, 109–10; Maness, *An Untutored Genius*, 63; *O.R.*, Series I, Part I, Vol. 10, 453–58; *Confederate Veteran* 9 (1901): 532.
40. Margaret Kelley Diary, June 6, 1862; Daniel, *Shiloh*, 296–97.
41. Both the reports of April 10 and April 19 are found in D.C. Kelley's service record, located in the Tennessee State Library and Archives.
Kelley is mistaken in saying Forrest was wounded on Sunday. Forrest fought at Fallen Timbers and was wounded there on Tuesday, April 8, 1862. The story of Forrest using a Union soldier, swooped up from the ground, is often told, but no firsthand documentation of the event is known.
Hospitals usually contained casualties from a single unit and were thus known by the name of the officer commanding that unit. On occasion, the hospital was designated by the name of the state from which the majority of its cases came; hence, Hardee's Hospital, Arkansas Hospital.
42. *Confederate Veteran* 6 (1898): 24.
43. Bradley, *Nathan Bedford Forrest's Escort*, 37; Rootsweb.ancestry.com, "Cowan"; Visitcowan.com/Cowan Family.
44. *O.R.*, Series I, Part I, Vol. 16, 820–29; Elmspringscsa.com, "General Frank Armstrong"; Civilwarstlouis.com, "Rock Champion."

CHAPTER 3

1. Kelley service record.
2. Ibid. Endorsements are on the back of the documents prepared by Kelley.
3. Margaret Kelley Diary, August 18, 24, 25, 1862; September 7, 25, 27, 1862; October 1, 9, 10, 11, 1862.
4. gordonwok/Heathenland.html, "Kate in a Heathen Land: A Sketch of Kate Lambuth written by her father." On his return to China, Charles

Marshall began to preach and became the first person of Chinese ancestry to be ordained as a minister by the Methodist Church. Later he studied medicine and became the superintendent of the hospital at the Methodist Mission in Soochow, China.

5. Margaret Kelley Diary, October 28; November 12, 23; December 13, 1862; *Huntsville Confederate*, May 18, 1863.

6. Margaret Kelley Diary, September 11, 1863; John Johnson Papers, MF 824, Reel5, Box 13.

7. Morgan, *How It Was*, 122.

8. *Confederate Veteran* 5 (1897): 101–2; *O.R.*, Series I, Vol. 39, Part 1, 786–87.

9. Kelley service record. All correspondence is included in the record.

10. Wyeth, *That Devil Forrest*, 349; Bearss, *Forrest at Brice's Cross Roads*, discusses the reorganization and training of Forrest's command in part I, chapters 2 and 3.

11. *Confederate Veteran* 8 (1900): 237.

12. *O.R.*, Series 1, Vol. 39, Part 2, 543, 717.

13. Bradley, *With Blood and Fire*, 11.

14. Bearss, *Forrest at Brice's Cross Roads*, 147, 151.

15. The history of the Escort and their relationship with David C. Kelley is recorded in Bradley, *Nathan Bedford Forrest's Escort*.

16. Bearss, *Forrest at Brice's Cross Roads*, 155; *O.R.*, Series 1, Vol. 39, Part 1, 318.

17. Bearss, *Forrest at Brice's Cross Roads*, 168; Hurst, *Nathan Bedford Forrest*, 200.

18. Bearss, *Forrest at Brice's Cross Roads*, 154–55.

19. Ibid., 211, 214.

20. *O.R.*, Series 1, Vol. 39, Part 1, 253; Bearss, *Forrest at Brice's Cross Roads*, 227–28.

21. *O.R.*, Series 1, Vol. 39, Part 1, 397.

22. *Confederate Veteran* 22 (1914): 556–57.

23. *O.R.*, Series I, Vol. 39, Part 1, 393, 398; Bearss, *Forrest at Brice's Cross Roads*, 276–77.

24. *O.R.*, Series 1, Vol. 39, Part 1, 398; Bearss, *Forrest at Brice's Cross Roads*, 303.

25. *O.R.*, Series 1, Vol. 39, Part 1, 399.

26. *Confederate Veteran* 34 (1926): 135; *O.R.*, Series 1, Vol. 39, Part 1, 542.

27. *O.R.*, Series 1, Vol. 39, Part 1, 518, 520–23, 542–43.

28. Ibid., 543–44; *Confederate Veteran* 34 (1926): 136; Duncan, *Recollections of a Confederate Soldier*, 165; Mathes, *General Forrest*, 287.

29. Duncan, *Recollections of a Confederate Soldier*, 169–70.

30. *O.R.*, Series 1, Vol. 39, Part 1, 544–45.

31. Bordon Berg, "Black Soldier Rides with 'Devil Forrest," *Washington Times*, August 7, 2008.

Holland lived in Murfreesboro, Tennessee, after the war. His home was located on what is today the Stones River National Battlefield. He is buried in a family cemetery just a few feet from the graves that are part of Hazen's Monument.

As a prisoner of war, Eli Lilly was sent to Enterprise, Mississippi, where he was allowed to give his parole not to escape. He ate with a family of the town and slept with the other paroled officers in a warehouse. A rumor reached Enterprise that a group of men from Jones County, Mississippi, a lawless area called "The Republic of Jones," intended to raid Enterprise and kill the Union prisoners there. Appealing to the Confederate provost, who had only a dozen old men and boys under his command, Lilly and twenty-five of his fellow officers were issued weapons and joined with their guards in patrolling the approaches to Enterprise until they were assured that the "army" from Jones was not really on its way. Lilly was later exchanged and found, on his release, that he had been promoted while a prisoner.

32. *O.R.*, Series 1, Vol. 39, Part 1, 545.

33. Ibid.; *Confederate Veteran* 34 (1926): 137; *Confederate Veteran* 6 (1898): 529. After the war, the Kentucky veterans of the engagement at Tarpley's Shop were successful in having the mass grave of their fallen comrades marked. The plot of land where the men are buried was deeded to the United Daughters of the Confederacy, and the plot is still cared for.

34. *O.R.*, Series 1, Vol. 39, Part 1, 546, 549.

35. Ibid., 539–40, 548.

36. Ibid., 540–41, 548; *Confederate Veteran* 5 (1897): 13. *Key West* was a wooden stern-wheel steamer. *Undine* was built at Cincinnati in 1863 and was purchased by the U.S. Navy. In July 1864, it had hit a snag in the river at Clifton, Tennessee, and sank. Refloated in August, *Undine* went to Paducah for repairs after Eastport. It and *Key West* would both meet Forrest's command again in just a few days in the Johnsonville expedition. John Darrough, Company F, 113th Illinois, was awarded the Congressional Medal of Honor for his action "saving the life of a captain" at Eastport.

37. Wyeth, *That Devil Forrest*, 456; Mathes, *General Forrest*, 297.

38. *O.R.*, Series 1, Vol. 39, Part 1, 873; Wyeth, *That Devil Forrest*, 460; *Confederate Veteran* 3 (1895): 78; Dinkins, *1861–1865 by an Old Johnnie*, 204.

39. *O.R.*, Series 1, Vol. 39, Part 1, 875; Wyeth, *That Devil Forrest*, 468–69.

40. *O.R.*, Series 1, Vol. 45, Part 1, 751–52; Mathes, *General Forrest*, 307–8; Bradley, *Nathan Bedford Forrest's Escort*, 1216–27. Fouche Springs is today called Summertown, Tennessee.

41. Jordan and Pryor, *Campaigns of General Nathan Bedford Forrest*, 618–19.

42. *O.R.*, Series 1, Vol. 45, Part 1, 753–55. Forrest did not file a report of combat losses in the cavalry at Franklin, but Chalmers had lost 116 men since entering the state more than a week earlier.

43. Groom, *Shrouds of Glory*, 229.

44. Mathes, *General Forrest*, 314–15; Fisher, *They Rode with Forrest*, 162. "Kelley's Point" is today part of the Nashville City Parks and Greenway system. A historical marker relates some of what took place there in December 1864.

45. Sword, *Confederacy's Last Hurrah*, 283–84.

46. Smith, "Le Roy Fitch Meets the Devil's Parson," 42–43.

47. Ibid., 47–48; Sword, *Confederacy's Last Hurrah*, 283.

48. Smith, "Le Roy Fitch Meets the Devil's Parson," 50; Sword, *Confederacy's Last Hurrah*, 284; *Confederate Veteran* 6 (1898): 436. The quartermaster of *Neosho*, John Dizenback, was awarded the Congressional Medal of Honor for going onto the exposed deck and replacing the national flag when the flagstaff was shot down. *Neosho* was a single-turret ironclad river monitor built at Carondelet, Missouri, in 1863. It was renamed *Vixen* in June 1869 and had that name changed to *Osceola* in August of the same year. It was sold for scrap in August 1873.

49. Sword, *Confederacy's Last Hurrah*, 303–4; 313–14.

50. Groom, *Shrouds of Glory*, 239, 243–45; *Confederate Veteran* 13 (1905): 30. The rail cut is still in use at the point where the USCT were trapped by it. It is about twenty-five feet in depth and more than twenty feet in width. The sides are sheer. The Confederates had constructed fieldworks to protect their position. A small portion of these, a lunette occupied during the battle by the three hundred survivors of Granbury's Brigade, still stands and is under permanent easement to the Sons of Confederate Veterans.

51. Groom, *Shrouds of Glory*, 246–48; Sword, *Confederacy's Last Hurrah*, 353. The "hinge" in the Confederate line was near the present location of Woodmont Christian Church and Woodmont Baptist Church, at the corner of Hillsboro and Woodmont. The main line ran roughly east from the present locations of the churches, and the detached redoubts were scattered to the south along Hillsboro Pike. Much of the area protected by the redoubts is now occupied by the Green Hills Mall.

52. Groom, *Shrouds of Glory*, 257–58; Sword, *Confederacy's Last Hurrah*, 364. "Peach Orchard Hill" is sometimes called "Overton Hill." The road that today connects Peach Orchard Hill with Shy's Hill and Hillsboro Pike is called Battery Lane. There is a small park atop Shy's Hill.

53. *Confederate Veteran* 13 (1905): 29; Fisher, *They Rode with Forrest*, 170–71; Sword, *Confederacy's Last Hurrah*, 367–68.

54. *O.R.*, Series 1, Vol. 45, Part 1, 757–58. Since Forrest was not at Nashville, his official report makes only a brief mention of what Chalmers's brigade did there.

55. *O.R.*, Series 1, Vol. 49, Part 1, 933, 972; Kelley, service record; Wyeth, *That Devil Forrest*, 513–14; Jordan and Pryor, *Campaigns of General Nathan Bedford Forrest*, 656.

56. Warner, *Generals in Gray*, 42.
57. Jordan and Pryor, *Campaigns of General Nathan Bedford Forrest*, 658.
58. Hughes, *General Tyree H. Bell*, 225–27; *O.R.*, Series 1, Vol. 49, Part 1.
59. Kelley, service record; Hughes, *General Tyree H. Bell*, p. 229; Fisher, *They Rode with Forrest*, 205–7.

CHAPTER 4

1. Tigert, *Bishop McTyeire*, 150–52.
2. Church Service Record of David Campbell Kelley; West, *Tennessee Encyclopedia of History*, "William Bowen Campbell," by John H. Thweatt; Margaret Lavinia Kelley to Mary Owen Campbell Kelley, September 6, 1884. Box 34, Campbell Papers; Margaret Lavinia Kelley to Mary Owen Campbell Kelley, September 8, 1884. Box 34, Campbell Papers; Mary Owen Campbell Kelley to Virginia Campbell, January 1, 1885. Box 34, Campbell Papers.
3. Farish, *Circuit Rider Dismounts*, 92.
4. Conkin, *Gone With the Ivy*, 8.
5. Tigert, *Bishop McTyeire*, 158.
6. Farish, *Circuit Rider Dismounts*, 265.
7. Conkin, *Gone With the Ivy*, 7; Farish, *Circuit Rider Dismounts*, 269–70; *Christian Advocate*, October 18, 1890.
8. Tigert, *Bishop McTyeire*, 174–77.
9. Conkin, *Gone With the Ivy*, 10.
10. Tigert, *Bishop McTyeire*, 178.
11. Ibid., 190.
12. Conkin, *Gone With the Ivy*, 17.
13. Farish, *Circuit Rider Dismounts*, 35.
14. Ibid., 223–24. As to the evolving racial views of Forrest, see Hurst, *Nathan Bedford Forrest*.
15. Farish, *Circuit Rider Dismounts*, 187.
16. Ibid., 189, 199; *Christian Advocate*, October 20, 1883.
17. Farish, *Circuit Rider Dismounts*, 204–5.
18. Alexander Winchell, "Science Gagged in Nashville," *Daily American*, June 16, 1878.
19. *Christian Advocate*, "The Vanderbilt Commencement," June 1, 1878.
20. Tigert, *Bishop McTyeire*, 220–21; Winchell, "Science Gagged in Nashville."
21. Kelley, "Letter to the Editor," *Christian Advocate*, March 3, 1878.
22. www.cinematreasures.org/Vendome. The Nashville public library now occupies the site of the theater, which burned in 1967.
23. *New York Times*, "Emma Abbott's Life Story," January 5, 1891.

24. *Daily American*, "Dr. Candler's Sermon Against the Play House," October 10, 1887.
25. Martin, *Emma Abbott*.
26. *Daily American*, "Miss Abbott Talks," October 10, 1887. Emma Abbott died of pneumonia in Salt Lake City on January 5, 1891. She left an estate of $500,000.
27. *Daily American*, "Letter to the Editor," October 12, 1887.
28. See *Christian Advocate*, October 22, October 29, November 12, December 3, 1887. Warren Akin Candler (1857–1941) left Nashville in 1888 to become president of Emory College. He helped transform that institution into a university and moved its location from Oxford, Georgia, to Atlanta. He rose to become a bishop in the Methodist Episcopal Church, South, and opposed reunification with the Northern branch of the church in 1939.
29. *Christian Advocate*, November 22, 1890.
30. Ibid., November 29, 1890.
31. Ibid., November 22, 1890.
32. Ibid.
33. Ibid.
34. Ibid., November 15, 1890; Mary Owen Campbell Kelley to ?, November 6, 1885. Box 34, Campbell Papers; Mary Owen Campbell Kelley to ?, November 11, 1885. Box 34, Campbell Papers. Both these letters are addressed to "Dear Friend."
35. *Christian Advocate*, December 6, 1890.
36. Ibid., May 16, 1891; *New York Times*, May 13, 1891.
37. Fisher, *They Rode with Wheeler*, 244–45.
38. *Christian Advocate*, May 31, 1894.

CHAPTER 5

1. *Confederate Veteran* 4 (1896): 475.
2. *Confederate Veteran* 5 (1897): 2, 157.
3. Bradley, *Nathan Bedford Forrest's Escort*, 139.
4. Pamphlet, *Dedication of Fort Donelson Memorial Chapel.* Box 44, Campbell Papers; statement by Steve Settle to author, July 3, 2010. The pulpit Bible was returned to the church in 1928 by the family of the U.S. soldier who took it. The Bible is on display at the church; statement by Steve Settle, historian of Fort Donelson Memorial Chapel, to author, July 4, 2010. The 1897 building burned in 1948 and was replaced by the current building, which stands on the same lot.
5. *Confederate Veteran* 8 (1900): 116, 154, 237, 391.

6. David C. Kelley, "General Nathan Bedford Forrest," *Methodist Review* (March–April 1900): 220–35.

7. *Confederate Veteran* 9 (1901): 94c; Bradley, *Nathan Bedford Forrest's Escort*, 187–88.

8. *Confederate Veteran* 13 (1905): 205, 389–90; pamphlet, *The Forrest Monument: Its History and Dedication*, 68–69. In possession of the author.

9. *Confederate Veteran* 14 (1906): 441; *Confederate Veteran* 16 (1908): 566; Bradley, *Nathan Bedford Forrest's Escort*, 190–92.

10. *Confederate Veteran* 16 (1908): xxvi–xxvii.

11. *Confederate Veteran* 9 (1901): 109.

12. *Sumner County News*, May 20, 1909.

13. *Confederate Veteran* 17 (1909): 421. The obituary is in error on some points. Neither Forrest nor Kelley was at the Battle of Murfreesboro; neither did Kelley ever hold a formal appointment as chaplain under Forrest. He may have been an aide in the early months of 1864 before resuming full duties as a combat officer.

Bibliography

Bearss, Edwin C. *Forrest at Brice's Cross Roads and in North Mississippi in 1864.* Dayton, OH: Press of Morningside Bookshop, 1994.

Blanton, J.C. "Forrest's Old Regiment." *Confederate Veteran* 3 (1895).

Bradley, Michael R. *Nathan Bedford Forrest's Escort and Staff.* Gretna, LA: Pelican Publishing Company, 2006.

———. *With Blood and Fire: Behind Union Lines in Middle Tennessee, 1863–65.* Shippensburg, PA: Burd Street Press, 2003.

Campbell Family Papers. Rare Book and Manuscript Collection, Perkins Library, Duke University, Durham, North Carolina.

ChildrenofBlackDavidCampbell.com.

Christian Advocate. Tennessee State Library and Archives.

Church Service Record of David Campbell Kelley, Archives of the United Methodist Church, Nashville, Tennessee.

Civilwarstlouis.com.

Confederate Veteran. 40 vols.

Conkin, Paul K. *Gone With the Ivy: A Biography of Vanderbilt University.* Knoxville: University of Tennessee Press, 1985.

Cooling, Benjamin Franklin. *Forts Henry and Donelson: The Key to the Confederate Heartland.* Knoxville: University of Tennessee Press, 1987.

Corder Manuscript, in possession of author. This manuscript provided by Mr. Ronnie Mangrum.

Daily American. Tennessee State Library and Archives.

Daniel, Larry J. *Shiloh: The Battle That Changed the Civil War.* New York: Simon & Schuster, 1997.

Dinkins, James. *1861-1865 by An Old Johnnie.* Dayton, OH: Morningside Press, 1975.

Duncan, Thomas D. *Recollections of a Confederate Soldier.* Nashville, TN: McQuiddy Printing Company, 1922. Reprinted by Kessinger Publishing's Rare Reprints, 2008.

Durham, Walter. *Nashville: The Occupied City, 1862–63.* Knoxville: University of Tennessee Press, 2008. First edition, 1984.

Elmspringscsa.com.

Familytreemaker.genealogy.com. Descendants of Dennis Kelley. John T. Kelley.

Farish, Hunter Dickinson. *The Circuit Rider Dismounts: A Social History of Southern Methodism, 1865–1900.* Richmond, VA: Dietz Press, 1938.

Fisher, John E. *They Rode with Forrest and Wheeler.* Jefferson, NC: McFarland & Co., Inc., 1995.

Groom, Winston. *Shrouds of Glory: From Atlanta to Nashville—The Last Great Campaign of the Civil War.* New York: Atlantic Monthly Press, 1995.

Historicnashville.org/vendometheatre.

Hughes, Nathaniel Chearis, Jr. *General Tyree H. Bell, CSA. Forrest's Fighting Lieutenant*. Knoxville: University of Tennessee Press, 2004.

Huntsville Confederate. Heritage Room Collection, Huntsville-Madison County Public Library.

Huntsville Democrat. Heritage Room Collection, Huntsville-Madison County Public Library.

Hurst, Jack. *Men of Fire: Grant, Forrest, and the Campaign That Decided the Civil War*. New York: Basic Books, 2007.

————. *Nathan Bedford Forrest: A Biography*. New York: Alfred A. Knopf, 1993.

Johnson, John Papers. MF824. Nashville: Tennessee State Library and Archives.

Jordan, Thomas, and J.P. Pryor. *The Campaigns of General Nathan Bedford Forrest*. New York: Da Capo Press, 1996. Original edition, 1869.

Kelley, David Campbell Church Service Record. Archives, United Methodist Church, Nashville, Tennessee.

Kelley, David Campbell Military Service Record. Tennessee State Library and Archives, Nashville, Tennessee.

Kelley, Lizzie Manney. "Memoirs of a Seventeen Year Old." Typescript in possession of the author.

Kelley, Margaret Lavinia Campbell Diary. Hargret Library Rare Books and Manuscript Collection, University of Georgia.

Kwok, Gordon, webmaster. "Kate in a Heathen Land." members.aol.com/ Gordonkwok/Heathenland.html.

Lindsley, John Berrien. *Military Annals of Tennessee. Confederate*. II Vols. Nashville: J. M. Lindsley & Co., 1886. Reprinted by Broadfoot Publishing Co., 1995.

Maness, Lonnie. *An Untutored Genius: The Military Career of Nathan Bedford Forrest.* Oxford, MS: Guild Bindery Press, 1990.

Martin, Sadie. *The Life and Professional Career of Emma Abbott.* Minneapolis, MN: L. Kimball Printing Co., 1891.

Mathes, J. Harvey. *General Forrest, Great Commanders Series.* New York: D. Appleton and Company, 1902.

Methodist Review, Hodges Library, University of Tennessee, Knoxville, Tennessee.

Morgan, Mrs. Irby. *How It Was: Four Years Among the Rebels.* Nashville: printed for the author by the Publishing House of the Methodist Episcopal Church, South, 1892.

Naval Historical Center. www.history.navy.mil.

New York Times. Online archives.

Official Records of the War of the Rebellion. Washington, D.C.: U.S. Government Printing Office, n.d.

Otey, Thomas G., and Gordon Kwok. "A Chinese Confederate Veteran and Methodist Missionary, Charles K. Marshall." Association to Commemorate the Chinese Serving in the American Civil War, Part 37. members.aol.com.gordonwok/cacwpart37.html.

Pilcher, Margaret Campbell. "Sketch of Captain David Campbell." *Tennessee Historical Quarterly* 8 (April 1903).

Rice, Charles. *Hard Times: The Civil War in Huntsville and North Alabama.* Huntsville, AL: Old Huntsville, 1994.

Slagle, Jay. *Ironclad Captain: Seth Ledyard Phelps and the U.S. Navy, 1841–1864.* Kent, OH: Kent University Press, 1996.

Smith, Myron J. "Le Roy Fitch Meets the Devil's Parson." *North & South Magazine* 10, no. 4.

Steenburn, Donald H. *The Man Called Gurley: N.B. Forrest's Notorious Captain.* Meredianville, AL: Elk River Press, 1999.

Sumner County News, 1909.

Sword, Wiley. *The Confederacy's Last Hurrah: Spring Hill, Franklin, Nashville.* Topeka: University Press of Kansas, 1992.

Thomason, John W., Jr. *Jeb Stuart.* New York: Charles Scribner's Sons, 1930.

Tigert, John J. *Bishop Holland Nimmons McTyerie.* Nashville, TN: Vanderbilt University Press, 1955.

Visitcowan.com.

Warner, Ezra J. *Generals in Gray.* Baton Rouge: Louisiana State University Press, 1959.

West, Carroll Van, ed. *The Tennessee Encyclopedia of History and Culture.* Nashville, TN: Rutledge Hill Press, 1998.

Wyeth, John Allen. "Appearance and Characteristics of Forrest." *Confederate Veteran* 4 (1896).

————. *That Devil Forrest: A Life of General Nathan Bedford Forrest.* Baton Rouge: Louisiana State University Press, 1989.

Index

About the Author

Michael R. Bradley earned his PhD from Vanderbilt University and taught U.S. history for thirty-six years at Motlow College in Tullahoma, Tennessee. Now professor emeritus, he remains an active author and speaker. He has written a number of Civil War books in addition to this biography of David C. Kelley.

Dr. Bradley is a life member of the Sons of Confederate Veterans and is the immediate past commander of the Tennessee Division of the SCV.

He and his wife live in Tullahoma, Tennessee.

Visit us at
www.historypress.net